HABITS OF A BRAIN

MASTER MIND

UNLOCK THE UNLIMITED POTENTIAL THAT YOU POSSESS WITHIN YOU

LEWIS KING

Table of Contents

PART 1 5

Chapter 1: How To Succeed In Life.......................................6

Chapter 2: Structure Your Day With Tasks You Excel At and Enjoy ..10

Chapter 3: *The People You Need in Your Life*..........................12

Chapter 4: Setting Too High Expectations...............................15

Chapter 5: *Don't Be Demotivated By Fear*................................18

Chapter 6: Overcoming Your Fears 21

Chapter 7: 7 Ways To Remove Excess Noise In Your Life..................24

Chapter 8: 7 Ways On How To Expect Change For The Better In Your Life...30

Chapter 9: 7 Habits That Are Good For You..............................34

Chapter 10: How to Identify the Obstacles Holding You Back...........39

PART 2 44

Chapter 1: *How to Determine What Makes You Happy* 45

Chapter 2: 6 Steps To Get Out of Your Comfort Zone 48

Chapter 3: 6 Concerning Effects of Mood On Your Life...................54

Chapter 4: How to Acknowledge The Unhappy Moments?.....................59

Chapter 5: Becoming High Achievers 63

Chapter 6: 10 Habits to Start Right Now.................................67

Chapter 7: *6 Ways To Get People To Like You*...........................73

Chapter 8: 8 Habits That Help You Live Longer.........................77

Chapter 9: Do More of What Already Works..............................82

Chapter 10: Deal With Your Fears Now 85

PART 3 88

Chapter 1: Creating Successful Habits 89

Chapter 2: 10 Habits That Damage Your Brain 93

Chapter 3: 10 Habits of Happy People 98

Chapter 4: 8 Habits That Can Make You Happy 103

Conclusion 107

Chapter 5: 6 Ways On How To Change Your Body Language To
Attract Success 108

Chapter 6: *5 Ways To Focus on Creating Positive Actions* 112

Chapter 7: *Five Habits That Make You Age Faster* 116

Chapter 8: 4 Ways Geniuses Come Up with Great Ideas 120

Chapter 9: Who Are You Working For? 124

Chapter 10: Playing To Your Strengths 127

PART 1

Chapter 1:

How To Succeed In Life

"You can't climb the ladder of success with your hands in your pocket."

Every day that you're living, make a habit of making the most out of it. Make a habit of winning today. Don't dwell on the past, don't worry about the future. You just have to make sure that you're winning today. Move a little forward every day; take a little step every day. And when you're giving your fruitful efforts, you're making sure you're achieving your day, then you start to built confidence within yourselves. Confidence is when you close your eyes at night and see a vision, a dream, a goal, and you believe that you're going to achieve it. When you're doing things, when you're productive the whole day, then that long journey will become short in a matter of time.

Make yourself a power list for each day. Take a sheet of paper, write Monday on top of it and then write five critical, productive, actionable tasks that you're going to do that day. After doing the task, cross it off. Repeat the process every day of every week of every month till you get closer to achieving your goals, your dreams. It doesn't matter if you're doing the same tasks every day or how minor or major they are; what matters is that it's creating momentum in things that you've believed you couldn't do. And as soon as the momentum gets completed, you start to believe that you can do something. You eventually stop writing your tasks down because now they've become your new habits. You need a reminder for them. You don't need to cross them off because you're going to do them. The power list helps you win the day. You're stepping out of your comfort zone, doing something that looks uncomfortable for starters, but while doing this, even for a year, you will see yourself standing five years from where you're standing today.

Decide, commit, act, succeed, repeat. If you want to be an inspiration to others, a motivator to others, impact others somehow, you have to self-evaluate certain perceptions and think that'll help you change the way you see yourself and the world. Perseverance, hard-working, and consistency would be the keywords if one were to achieve success in life. You just have to keep yourself focused on your ultimate goal. You will fall a hundred times. There's always stumbling on the way. But if you have the skill, the power, the instinct to get yourself back up every time you fall, and to dig yourself out of the whole, then no one can stop you. You have to control the situation, Don't ever let the situation control you. You're living life exactly as it should be. If you don't like what you're living in, then consider changing the aspects. The person you are right now versus the person you want to be in the future, there's only a fine line between the two that you have to come face-to-face with.

Your creativity is at most powerful the moment you open your eyes and start your day. That's when you get the opportunity to steer your emotions and thoughts in the direction that you want them to go, not the other way around. Every failure is a step closer to success. We won't succeed on the first try, and we will never have it perfect by trying it only once. But we can master the art of not giving up. We dare to take risks. If we never fail, we never get the chance of getting something we never had. We can never taste the fruits of success without falling. The difference between successful people and those who aren't successful is the point of giving up.

Success isn't about perfection. Instead, it's about getting out of bed each day, clearing the dust off you, and thinking like a champion, a winner, going on about your day, being productive, and making the most out of it. Remember that the mind controls your body; your body doesn't hold your mind. You have to make yourself mentally tough to overcome the fears and challenges that come in the way of your goals. As soon as you get up in the morning, start thinking about anything or anyone that you're grateful for. Your focus should be on making yourself feel good and confident enough to get yourself through the day.

The negative emotions that we experience, like pain or rejection, or frustration, cannot always make our lives miserable. Instead, we can consider them as our most incredible friends that'll drive us to success. When people succeed, they tend to party. When they fail, they tend to ponder. And the pondering helps us get the most victories in our lives. You're here, into another day, still breathing fine, that means you got another chance, to better yourself, to be able to right your wrongs. Everyone has a more significant potential than the roles they put themselves in.

Trust yourself always. Trust your instinct—no matter what or how anyone thinks. You're perfectly capable of doing things your way. Even if they go wrong, you always learn something from them. Don't ever listen to the naysayers. You've probably heard a million times that you can't do this and you can't do that, or it's never even been done before. So what? So what if no one has ever done it before. That's more of the reason for you to do it since you'll become the first person to do it. Change that 'You can't' into 'Yes, I definitely can.' Muhammad Ali, one of the greatest boxers to walk on the face of this planet, was once asked, 'how many sit-ups do you do?' to which he replied, 'I don't count my sit-ups. I only start counting when it starts hurting. When I feel pain, that's when I start counting because that's when it really counts.' So we get a wonderful lesson to work tirelessly and shamelessly if we were to achieve our dreams. Dr. Arnold Schwarzenegger beautifully summed up life's successes in 6 simple rules; Trust yourself, Break some rules, Don't be afraid to fail, Ignore the naysayers, Work like hell, And give something back.

Chapter 2:

Structure Your Day With Tasks You Excel At and Enjoy

Today's video will probably appeal to people who have a say in the way they can structure their day. People who are working on their own businesses, or are freelancers. But it could also apply to those with full time jobs if your jobs allow flexibility.

For those who have been doing their own thing for a while, we know that it is not easy to put together a day that is truly enjoyable. We forget about doing the things we like and excel at, and start getting lost in a sea of work that we have to drag ourselves through doing.

If we don't have a choice, then I guess we can't really do anything about it. But if we do, we need to start identifying the tasks that require the most attention but the least effort on our part to do. Tasks that seem just about second-nature to us. Tasks that we would do even if nobody wanted to pay us. Tasks that allow our creativity to grow and expand, tasks that challenge us but not drain us, tasks that enriches us, or tasks that we simply enjoy doing.

The founding father of modern Singapore, one of the wealthiest countries in the world, Mr Lee Kuan Yew once said, find what works and just keep doing it over and over again. I would apply that to this situation as well. We have to find what works for us and just double down on it. The other stuff that we aren't good at, either hire someone else to do it, or find a way to do less of it or learn how to be good at it fast. Make it a challenge for ourselves. Who knows maybe you might find them enjoyable once you get a hang of it as well.

But for those things that already come naturally to us, do more of it. Pack a lot of time into at the start of the day. Dedicated a few hours of your day to those meaningful tasks that you excel at. You will find that once you get the creative juices and the momentum going, you will be able to conquer the other less pleasing tasks more easily knowing that you've already accomplished your goals for the day.

Start right now. Identify what those tasks that you absolutely love to do right now, work-wise, or whatever it may be, and just double down on it. Watch your day transform.

Chapter 3:

The People You Need in Your Life

We all have friends, the people that are there for us and would be there no matter what. These people don't necessarily need to be different, and these traits might all be in one person. Friends are valuable. You only really ever come across ones that are real. In modern-day society, it's so hard to find friends that want to be your friends rather than just to use you.

Sometimes the few the better, but you need some friends that would guide you along your path. We all need them, and you quite possibly have these traits too. Your friends need you, and you may not even know it.

1. The Mentor

No matter which area or field they are trying to excel in, the common denominator is that they have clarity about life and know exactly what their goals are. These people can impact you tremendously, helps you get into the winners' mindset, infuse self-belief and confidence in you then you, too, can succeed and accomplish your goals. They act as a stepping stone for you to get through your problems. They are happy for your success and would guide you through the troubles and problems while trying to get there.

2. Authentic People

You never feel like you have to make pretense around these people. Life can be challenging enough, so having friends that aren't judging you and are being themselves is very important for your well-being. This type of friend allows you to be vulnerable, express your emotion in healthy ways, and helps bring a smile back to your face when you're down.

They help you also show your true self and how you feel. Rather than showing only a particular side of their personality, they open their whole self to you, allowing you to do the same and feel comfortable around them.

3. Optimists

These people are the kind you need, the ones that will encourage you through tough times. They will be there encouraging you, always seeing the best in the situation. Having the ability to see the best in people and will always have an open mind to situations. Everyone needs optimism in their lives, and these people bring that.

"Optimism is essential to achievement, and it is also the foundation of courage and true progress." -Nicholas M. Butler.

4. Brutally Honest People

To have a balanced view of yourself and be aware of your blind spots is important for you. Be around people who would provide authentic feedback and not sugarcoat while giving an honest opinion about you. They will help you be a better version of yourself, rectifying your mistakes, work on your weak spots, and help you grow. These are the people you can hang around to get better, and you will critique yourself but in a good way, helping you find the best version of yourself. Of course, the ones that are just rude should be avoided, and they should still be nice to you but not too nice to the point where they compliment you even when they shouldn't.

Chapter 4:

Setting Too High Expectations

Today we're going to talk about the topic of setting too high expectations. Expectations about everything from work, to income, to colleagues, friends, partners, children, family. Hopefully by the end of this video I will be able to help you take things down a notch in some areas so that you don't always get disappointed when things don't turn out the way you expect it to.

Let's go one by one in each of these areas and hopefully we can address the points that you are actively engaged in at the moment.

Let's begin with work and career. Many of us have high expectations for how we want our work life to be. How we expect our companies and colleagues to behave and the culture that we are subjected to everyday. More often that not though, companies are in the business of profit-making and cutting costs. And our high expectations may not meet reality and we might end up getting let down. What I would recommend here is that we not set these expectations of our colleagues and bosses, but rather we should focus on how we can best navigate through this obstacle course that is put in front of us. We may want to focus instead on how we can handle ourselves and our workload. If however we find that we just can't shake off this expectations that we want from working in a company, maybe we want to look elsewhere to companies that have a work culture that suits our personality. Maybe one that is more vibrant and encourages freedom of expression.

Another area that we should address is setting high expectations of our partners and children. Remember that we are all human, and that every person is their own person. Your expectations of them may not be their expectations of themselves. When you impose such an ideal on them, it may be hard for them to live up to. Sure you should expect your partner to be there for you and for your children to behave a certain way. But beyond that everyone has their own personalities and their own thoughts and ideas. And what they want may not be in line with what we want for them. Many a times for Asian parents, we expect our kids to get good grades, get into good colleges, and maybe becoming a doctor or lawyer one day. But how many of us actually understand what our kids really want? How many of us actually listen to what our kids expect of themselves? Maybe they really want to be great at music, or a sport, or even finance. Who's to say what's actually right? We should learn to trust others and let go of some of our own expectations of them and let them become whoever they want to be.

The next area I want to talk about is simply setting too high expectations of yourself. Many times we have an ideal of who we want to be - how we want to look, how we want our bodies to look, and how we want our bank statement to look, amongst many others. The danger here is when we set unrealistic expectations as to when we expect these things to happen. Remember most things in life takes time to happen. The sooner you realise that you need more time to get there, the easier it will be on yourself. When we set unrealistic timelines, while it may seem ideal to rush through the process to get results fast, more often than not we are left disappointed when we don't hit them. We then get discouraged and may even feel like a failure or give up the whole process entirely. Wouldn't it be better if we could give ourselves more time for nature to work its magic? Assuming you follow the steps that you have laid out and the action plans you need to take, just stretch this timeline out a little farther to give yourself more breathing room. If you feel you are not progressing as fast as you had hoped, it is okay to seek help and to tweak your plans as they go along. Don't ever let your high expectations discourage you and always have faith and trust in the process even when it seems hard.

One final thing I want to talk about is how we can shift from setting too high expectations to one of setting far-out goals instead. There is a difference. Set goals that serve to motivate you and inspire you to do things rather than ones that are out of fear. When we say we expect something, we immediately set ourselves up for disappoint. However if we tell ourselves that we really want something, or that we want to achieve something that is of great importance to us, we shift to a goal-oriented mindset. One that is a lot healthier. We no longer fear the deadline creeping up on us. We instead continually work on getting there no matter how long it takes. That we tell ourselves we will get there no matter what, no matter how long. The key is to keep at it consistently and never give up.

Having the desire to work at an Apple store as a retail specialist, I never let myself say that I expect apple to hire me by a certain time otherwise I am never pursuing the job ever again. Rather I tell myself that being an Apple specialist is my dream job and that I will keep applying and trying and constantly trying to improve myself until Apple has no choice but to hire me one day. A deadline no longer bothers me anymore. While I wait for them to take me in, I will continue to pursue other areas of interest that will also move my life forward rather than letting circumstances dictate my actions. I know that I am always in control of my own ship and that I will get whatever I put my mind to eventually if I try hard enough.

So with that I challenge each and every one of you to be nicer to yourselves. Lower your lofty expectations and focus on the journey instead of the deadline. Learn to appreciate the little things around you and not let your ego get in the way.

I hope you learned something today, take care and I'll see you in the next one.

Chapter 5:

Don't Be Demotivated By Fear

What are you doing right now? What ambitions do you have for the morning to come? What doubts you have in mind? What is stopping you right now?

You have doubts about anything because you want to be cautious. You are hesitant because you have your gut telling you to think again. The reality is you are afraid and you don't know it. Or maybe you do know it but you keep ignoring your weakness.

That weakness you keep ignoring is your fear. Fear starts with a seed but if left alone can manifest deeper roots and can have a devastating impact on one's personality.

Fear is the biggest enemy of commitment. Fear kills productivity. Fear eats creativity. Fear crushes motivation.

People keep fears as if they are being smart about unexpected outcomes. You don't need to stay afraid of things to abstain from them. The only thing you need to fear is the 'Fear' itself.

When you were a child, your parents motivated you and gave you the confidence to get over most of your fears. But now you would be considered stupid and childish if you seek a mentor. You what do you do?

The answer is simple. You have yourself to try out things that make you take a step back. Because fear is self-imposed. You made yourself prone to such feelings and you can make them go away as well.

Fear can make you second guess your own abilities.

We are way behind our goals because subconsciously we have thought of the failure that can happen. The fear of our dreams shattering overtakes the ambition and happiness when you finally get to the scale. This overburdening feeling of fear keeps us sitting in our seats and stops us from trying out new things. This fear makes us believe that we don't deserve what we have dreamt of.

So I have a question for you! What have you done in the last week, or month or even a year to overcome only the smallest phobia?

If you haven't, it is possible that you won't leave what you have right now and never go for anything more than you can own. This reason is that fear makes you remain content with whatever nature and God have bestowed upon you on time after time. But you won't get up and try to work new things for bigger and better blessings that hard work and some gutsy calls have to offer.

If you can't give up the feeling of harm that might come if you finally decide to indulge in those reluctant goals, take a different approach then. Think of it as what can you be on that other side of the river? What colors does the other side of the canvas have? What laughs can you have if you made that one joke? What gains you can have if you increased just one pound?

If you try to make your fears a medium of self-analysis, maybe you start to gain the motivation that faded quickly with every second you spent in front of that source of fear. Then you might start to see a whole new image of your personality and this might be the person you always wish you could be!

Chapter 6:

Overcoming Your Fears

Today we're going to talk about the topic of fears. What fear is and how we can overcome it. Now before we dive into it, let us just take a brief moment to think of or right down what our greatest fears are right now.

Whether it be taking the next step in your relationship, fear of the unknown, fear of quitting your job and not finding another one, fear or death, fear of illnesses, whatever fear that jumps out at you and is just eating at you at the back of your mind, i want you to remember that fear as we go through this video.

So what is fear exactly? Whilst there are many definitions of fear out there, I'm going to take, as usual, my spin on things. And to me fear is simply a negative feeling that you assign to usually a task that you really don't want to do. And most of the time, the fear is of the unknown, that you can't visualise what is going to happen next. You don't know whether the outcome will be good or bad, and you don't know whether it is the right move to make. So this trio of thoughts keep circling round and round and eventually you just decide that you are not going to take any action on it and you just shove it to one side hoping that it goes away. And whilst you may do that temporarily, sometimes even for months, one day you are going to have to come face to face with it again. And when that day comes, you will either be paralysed again or you may again put it off to a later date.

We procrastinate on our fears because we want a sure thing. We want to know what will happen next, and we fear what we don't know.

Now for the fears that we are talking about today, it is something that will affect your life if u don't take action. If it is like a fear of bungee jumping or sky driving, sure that fear is physical and very real, but also you can make a choice not to do it and your problem is solved. It will not affect your life in a negative way if u don't do it.

But if it is a fear of a career switch because you already hate your job so much and are totally miserable, that is a fear that you should do your best to try and address as soon as possible.

So what can and should you do about these sorts of fears? The answer for this one is not going to be that difficult. Simply think of the consequences of not conquering your task and how much it might prevent you from moving forward in life and you have got your answer.

When the pain associated with not accomplishing the task becomes greater than the fear we assign to it, it is the tipping point that we need to finally take that action. But instead of waiting to get to that excruciating pain, we can visualise and project what it could potentially feel like if we don't do it now and the pain we might feel at a later day, say 1 year from now, when we have wasted another full year of our life not taking that leap of faith, the time we have burned, the time we can never get back, and the opportunity cost of not taking action now, we might just decide that we don;t want to wait until that day comes and face that huge amount of regret that we should've done something a lot sooner.

And what we need to simply do is to just take action. Taking action is something you will hear from all the gurus you will find out there. When faced with a fear or challenge, instead of wondering what dangers lurk in the unknown, just take action and let the experience tell you whether it was indeed the right or wrong decision. Do you necessary homework and due diligence beforehand and take that calculated step forward instead of procrastinating on it. Life is too short to be mucking around. Just go for it and never live your life in fear or regret ever again.

I challenge each and everyone of you to go through the list that we have created at the start of the video. The one that you have been most fearful of doing. And i want you to assess the pros and cons of each fear that you have written down. If there are more pros than cons, i want you to set a deadline for yourself that you will take action on it. And that deadline is today. Don't waste precious time worrying and instead spend more time doing.

I hope you learned something today and as always take care and i wish you all the best in overcoming your fears and achieving your goals as fast as possible. See you in the next one.

Chapter 7:

7 Ways To Remove Excess Noise In Your Life

Ever felt lost in a world that is so fast-paced, where no two moments are the same? Do you ever have a hard time achieving your goals, just because you have more distractions than a purpose to jump to success?

We live in a time, where technology is the biggest ease as well as the biggest difficulty while achieving our goals.

When you need something to be fixed, the internet can save us a lot of time, but the same internet can prove to be the biggest cause to take away the focus of the most determined too.

Although there are many important things on the internet too, that are essential to our daily lives, we don't need them at all times. Especially the realm of social media platforms.

Youtube, Facebook even Instagram can prove to be a beneficial tool for learning and teaching. But it can also make you spend more and more time on things that won't give you much except a good laugh here and there.

So what habits or activities can you adapt to distill these distractions. Reduce noise in life helping you focus better on the things that matter the most.

1. Divide your Tasks Into Smaller Ones

When you already have many distractions in life, including the household tasks and other daily life chores that you must attend to, then you must not avoid those.

But your dreams and goals must not be put aside at all, instead one must learn to complete them by dividing them into smaller, more manageable tasks.

Those who depend on you must have you when they need you, but that shouldn't stop you from doing what you require from yourself.

That can be done by keeping your head in the work whenever you get the chance to get maximum results from those short intervals.

2. Manage Your Time Smartly

Life is too short to be indulging in every whim and activity that you crave. Not everything or thought requires you to act upon.

A human being is the smartest being on this planet but also the stupidest. When a man or a woman wants to achieve something with all their heart, they do get it eventually. But when they have a thousand silly desires to go for, they slide off the set path as if there were none.

"You only Live Once".

Logically, this is a valid quote to get anyone off their path to success. But, realistically this is also the most common reason for the failure of a majority of our youngsters.

You only get this life once, So you must go for the acts that bring you a better future with a surety of freedom without having to rely on anyone. Life doesn't need to be a continuous struggle once you use your energies at the right time for the right time.

3. Get Your Head Out of Social Media

I know this may sound a little Grownup and cliched, but we spend more time on our mobiles and laptops than going out and doing something physically in all our senses with our actual hands.

We can believe and act on anything that pops up on this screen but rarely do we get anything worthwhile that we can adapt to change our lives once and for all.

Social media might be the new medium and source of knowledge and business for many, but for a layman, this is also the biggest waste of creative energy.

There is a lot out there to do in real life, a lot that we can realistically achieve. But, these days, we tend to hide behind a simple tweet and believe that we have done enough when the reality could have been much different.

4. Avoid Unhealthy Relationships

You might have always heard that a friend can be an emotional escape when you need one, but the excess of friends can prove to be the opposite of that. People seem to think, the more friends you have, the better you have a chance to stay engaged and have a happy social life. But this isn't always the case.

The more you have friends, your devotion gets scattered and you find solace in everyone's company. This makes you more exposed, and people might take advantage of that. The fewer friends you have, the better loyalty you can expect and better returns of a favor.

When you have fewer friends, even if you lose one someday or get deceived, you would require less time to bounce back from the incident and you won't have to worry for long.

5. Get Out of Home Environment

Productivity required a productive environment. People tend to look for ease, but it doesn't always help us with finding our true potential.

You sometimes need a strict office environment or a more organized station or workplace. A place where there is no distraction or source of wandering thoughts to get your attention.

People need to understand how our brains work. If you cannot focus sitting in your bed, get a chair and a table. If that doesn't work for you, take a stool without a backrest. If you still feel at ease, just pick a standing table and start working while standing on your feet.

This makes your mind stay more focused on the task at hand to be done quickly.

6. Make A Schedule For These Distractions

If you feel like you can't give up the urge to pick your phone and check your feed. Or if you need to watch the last quarter of the league, Or if you need to have a smoke.

Don't start fighting these urges. It won't help you, rather make things worse.

If you cannot let go off of these things, it's fine. Make a deal with your brain, that you need this last page done within the next 10 minutes, and then I can go do what I needed direly.

You have to come at peace with your mind and work as a single unit. So make time for these distractions and gradually you might be able to drop them once and for all.

7. You Don't Have to Compare With Anyone

Why do we humans need to compare and compete? Because we think it keeps our drive and our struggle alive. We think it gives us a reason and a purpose to go on and makes us see our goals more clearly.

Comparing to others won't make you see 'Your Goals', rather you would start creating goals that were never meant to be for you. You have these priorities just because you saw someone with something that appealed to you.

This is the noise and distraction that deviates you from the path that was meant to be for you all along.

If you want a clear vision of what you want, start removing cluttered thoughts, acts, and people from your life. It might seem hard at the start, but you won't have any regrets once everything comes in place.

Chapter 8:

7 Ways On How To Expect Change For The Better In Your Life

The quicker you accept the fact that change is inevitable and can't be avoided, the better off you will be. The change could be better or worse; if you want it to be the former, you need to take complete control of your life. As life moves on, it's logical that the more transition and change you go through, the more opportunity you will have to perceive the patterns of your life, whether you will be able to handle the change or not, or how you can successfully negotiate and navigate these necessary transitions. We can do many things to turn our lives around; we can adopt habits and ideologies that will make us successful, but more importantly, happy. Now, you know yourself well enough to know what you want, what you realistically can do, and ideally, how you can accomplish those ideas and plans. Here are some ways to expect change for the better in your life.

1. Find Meaning and Purpose

Finding meaning in your life is easier said than done. You need to understand that knowing one's specific purpose takes more time than one can imagine. Life does not always go according to our plan; there are loads of unexpected changes that we have to deal with on our way. Therefore, it is essential to understand the difference between goals and purposes; we often confuse these two. For example, you might think that your purpose is to become a famous athlete or scientist or even the president. However, these are merely your goals and not your purpose. Your purpose should be broader and more open than your ambitions or passions. It must positively impact the world or even be a key to your happiness and love.

2. Love and Respect Yourself

How can you expect to gain the respect and love of people when you can't even do that for yourself? To bring a positive evolution in your life, you need to build your self-confidence and self-esteem, which can only be achieved by working hard on yourself and taking action. Whether you face rejections or failures, accepting all the negativity and loving yourself regardless will help you move on more quickly. Putting yourself down and clinging to regrets will get you nowhere. As long as you love yourself and are satisfied with yourself, the opinions of others shouldn't matter to you.

3. Stop Making Excuses

This is a rule that you should embody in your soul; if you want to achieve something and bring positive change in your life, then you should stop lying to yourself. Understand that your time is limited, and the excuses you make will only waste it. Every explanation for failure is ultimately an excuse, and they do nothing but bring you down. Life isn't as easy as we see in the movies. Success and happiness can't be achieved in the blink of an eye. There will be many obstacles, and life will throw some serious curveballs at you. But what matters, in the end, is how we keep moving forward despite it all. Instead of making excuses and lying to ourselves for our failures, we should keep working hard.

4. Develop The Habit of Positive Thinking

It is said to believe that positive thoughts and confidence bring positive changes in our life. Sure, only thinking about it won't lead you to success, but it will motivate you and help you to give your absolute best. The law of attraction is proved to be somewhat true to many people. Therefore, we should try to be more optimistic and envision ourselves achieving our goals and working hard towards them. We should be in a positive mindset all the time; even if something negative happens to us, we should focus on the good more.

5. Develop A Productive Routine

Having a productive routine is essential for a successful life; it is critical to manage your time wisely and eventually turn all the positive things into your habits. Start with smaller tasks, like making your bed after getting up. This can actually give you positive reinforcement to start your day and eventually lead to a happy and productive day.

6. Set Goals For Yourself

You need to set some goals if you want to achieve anything worthwhile in your life. These goals are what keeps you motivated and helps you to stay on track. Set both short-term as well as long-term goals and work hard towards achieving them. Remember, your goals can change along the way; you have to be flexible about it and focus on giving your best effort in their pursuit.

7. Live A Healthy Lifestyle

If your physical health is good, your mental health will be good, and vice versa. Adopting a healthier lifestyle can bring positive changes in your physical as well as mental health. It can help you turn your life around. It is essential to take care of our diet and make sure to exercise regularly. Good health is vital for a happy and content life.

Conclusion

To sum it up, by following the above tips, you will have a tremendously positive result. You will be able to change your life for the better.

Chapter 9:

<u>7 Habits That Are Good For You</u>

The cognitive ability to distinguish what is good from what is bad for us is an invaluable skill. Cherry-picking nutritive habits in a world full of all manner of indecency comes handy especially if you want to stand out from the crowd.

Here are 7 habits that are good for you:

1. <u>Waking Up Early</u>

The early bird catches the worm. Early risers have the opportunity to pick the best for themselves before the rest of the world is awake. It is healthy and prudent to wake up early and start your day before most people do. You leverage on opening your business early before your competitors. Besides, the preparedness of early risers is unmatched even as the day progresses.

Waking up early is not a reserve for 'busy people' only. It is for everyone in this world of survival for the fittest. We all have 24 hours in one day. The difference comes from how we use our time. One may spend more than 8 hours sleeping and another will spend just 6 hours for the same. You cannot sleep as if you are competing with the dead and expect to make it in the land of the living.

Early risers are active people. They are as alert as chamois, prepared for any eventuality.

2. Associate With Successful People

Show me your friends and I will show you what kind of person you are. Success, like most things, is contagious. In his book *48 laws of power*, Robert Greene writes *'avoid the unhappy and unlucky.'* This is not discrimination. Association with the unhappy and unlucky will contaminate you with negative energy.

Associate with successful people and you will follow their example. You will emulate their saving culture, their investment behavior, and their aggressiveness in business. In the shadow of the successful, you will attract positivity and grow exponentially. Maintain knit relationships with the successful.

3. Be Teachable

A teachable spirit will take you places where your character will not. A teachable person is capable of receiving correction graciously without perceiving it as demeaning. Do not be afraid of getting things wrong. Instead, be worried when you lack the humility to accept correction.

Being teachable is one of the greatest strengths you can have. We all are a work in progress, never finished products. What happens when you refuse to be under the tutelage of the successful and experienced? The greatest lessons are not learned in a classroom but the school of life.

4. Accepting Challenges

When challenged by circumstances we face, be the bigger brother/sister. Take challenges positively and work towards a solution instead of whining about this or that. Our patience, skills, and competence are sometimes put to the test. A test so subtle that we fail without even realizing it. When you have a positive mindset of accepting challenges, you will ace the game. Prove your worth wherever you are through your actions, never by your words.

When you accept a challenge and conquer it, it takes you to another level. The beauty of life lies in progress with the assurance that change is a constant. Accept challenges towards positivity and not the dark ones. Ignore that which derails your purpose or goes against your principles.

5. Learn When To Retreat and To Advance

The art of knowing when to push or pull is important in life. On the battlefield, retreating and advancing by troops is a call their leader makes. He decides that for his team based on his training, the immediate situation, and his judgment. Retreating is not a sign of weakness; neither is advancing a sign of strength. Both are strategies to win a war.

It is okay to retreat from a cause you were pursuing or to adjust your plans. Just make it worth your while. When you resume, be stronger than before. Again, when you retreat, do not succumb to the ridicule of your enemies when they mistake it for weakness. The fear of what the opinion of others (non-entities) is should not make you afraid of retreating to strategize.

When you make up your mind to advance with a noble course, advance skillfully. Do not advance blindly or ignorant of what you intend to achieve. Train your focus on the target.

6. Ask for help.

We are mortals; facing deficiencies here and there. We do not always have the answer to everything. Ask for help from the knowledgeable ones when in a quagmire.

Asking for help is not a weakness. It is appreciating the strengths of others. It is also appreciating the diversity of the human race that we are not endowed with everything. The silent rule is that you should be careful whom you approach for help. Some ill-intentioned people will sink you deep into trouble.

Nevertheless, asking for help is perfectly normal and it is something you should try sometimes. When you ask for help from the experienced, you save yourself the trouble of making messy mistakes. Learn through others who trod down the same road. Their lessons are invaluable; you will avoid their mistakes.

7. <u>Develop hobbies.</u>

Hobbies are those things you engage in for fun. They are very important because you take a break from your daily hustles. In your hobbies, you are carefree. You do not have to worry about your boss or business partners.

Hobbies are meant to be fun. If you are not having fun when doing your hobbies, probably they are no longer one. You should consider finding new ones. All work without play makes Jack a dull boy.

Hobbies are good for you. Go for swimming or that road trip, find a sport and play for fun, go beyond singing in the shower, travel everywhere you desire, or even start watching that TV series you are always curious about. Variety is the spice of life. Do not be afraid to spice up your life with all that your heart desires.

The above 7 habits are good for you. They will help you grow and increase your productivity in all you do.

Chapter 10:
How to Identify the Obstacles Holding You Back

Hi everyone! Have you ever wanted something in your life so badly but you failed to take any action to get it? Did you ever find out what was holding you back?

As humans, we have lots of aspirations and dreams. We strive to be rich and successful, pursuing our passions, having a big family, and living in a nice house with our dream car.
But how many of us were able to chase down that dream?

In today's video, we're going to talk about just that.

Let's find out how you can identify the obstacles holding us back from achieve your goals and how you can overcome them.

Before we begin, I would like you to first think about a goal you've been wanting to achieve but haven't started working on. If you're insightful, then ask yourself what are the possible reasons holding you back from working on it. Why are you procrastinating? Now that you've got something to latch on to, we can start to deconstruct the issues you might be facing.

1. Fear of Failure

Most of the time, fear holds us back. Fear of failure is the most common fear that stops many people, including you and me, from working towards our intended goals. We are so afraid to fail after putting in an enormous amounts of time and effort, but we fail to realise that falling down is part of the process to victory. We do not see the struggles that many successful people have had to go through to get to where they are today – we only see the dollar signs that are tied to their name, their net-worth, their fancy houses and cars, things that are on face value. But in reality, they have had to fail their way to success. And we are oblivious to their trials and tribulations, their mindset, their incredible work ethic, and their ability to get themselves back up after falling flat on their faces and try again.

2. Fear of Change

Another fear that could be holding you back from taking action is the fear of change. You may find it challenging to go out of your comfort zones to explore the big world of possibilities waiting for you. You may find your current position very safe, warm, and cosy. No stress, no pressure, just simply fine. But there's no growth in your comfort zone.

I am here to tell you that going out there to try new things isn't going to be easy. There may be a steep learning curve and a huge mountain waiting for you to climb. Are you willing to step out of that perfectly warmed home into a blizzard outside?

Putting yourself in uncomfortable situations is the only way that you will face challenges that might prove to be rewarding in the long run. Changes that will give you new perspectives and teach you new lessons that you wouldn't have learnt otherwise if you merely stay in your safe zone. So don't be afraid to go out in the world and try new things. No matter what the outcome is, the experiences you'll gain along the way will always be priceless.

3. Fear of Judgement

Fear of being judged for doing things that are out of the norm is something that many of us are afraid of. In today's world, society has created a frame and a timeline of what seems to be pleasing and acceptable. Without realising it, we have been gradually moulded by society to try our best to blend into the crowd, not stand out. You may also inevitably feel that same pressure to simply just fit in. This irrational fear of being judged by others, whether it be our friends, family members, or even complete strangers, stops us in doing what we really want to do.

Now try to imagine yourself in a situation where other people won't judge you no matter what your dreams are. Instead, they will celebrate you for taking action and chasing your passions in life. If that were the reality, what will you do?

By reframing our thoughts, instead of succumbing to our desires of trying please everyone around us, we are thinking for ourselves first for once. There is no fear of judgement of pursuing what really matters to us. Don't be afraid to go out of that frame and restart. Listen to your own intuition and don't let the world put your hands on you and crush your dreams.

4. Fear of Making Mistakes

Are you the kind that always aces your test at school when you were young without studying? Or did you do well in school because you practiced a thousand times over before finally getting it right when it comes exam time?

You might think that having the perfect plan or having the perfect strategy is essential before you can begin executing your dreams, but in reality, a lot of the success only comes over time after many trials and errors. We have to keep the mindset that we will figure things out along the way as we travel down that new path. The journey will not be smooth sailing no matter how perfect we can try to make our plans to be. As with failures, making mistakes is part of the game. It is how you react to and manage the problems that come up that will be the true test of your capabilities.

Perfectionism is a trap that stops us from doing what we want. Doing something imperfectly is so much better than not doing anything at all because of the fear of imperfection.

5. Having a Weak Mindset

Another factor that holds people back is their own mindset. Have you ever wanted to try something out but you instantly think that you can't do it? The thought that you are incapable of something is all in your mind. You must tell yourself that you are flexible and fluid. That you are able to achieve anything you set your mind to.

That you have what it takes to go after the life that you want. The truth is, you have everything within you to be successful if you'll just believe that you can. Every time you catch yourself thinking that you can't be who you want to be, the reality is not that you can't do it, but rather that you just simply don't want to do it – either out of laziness or out of the fears that we have described so far.

To change your life you first have to change your mindset and be open to all possibilities.

6. Blaming Others Your Shortcomings

It is human nature to blame others for things that we lack or fail to do. We may direct our failure to take action to our circumstances, our environment, our lack of resources, or even our parents.

Blaming everything and everyone around you for your circumstances will hinder you from moving forward. Instead, be accountable for your own progress. We all have a choice to look at ourselves first and find the shortcomings that we may have. It could be a lack of motivation, lack of perseverance, , lack of patience, lack of consistency, and lack of discipline that is holding you back.

It is time to stop looking at external factors as reasons for our inability to take action. We all need to start working on ourselves first before we can see real change and progress happen to our lives. If you don't want where you are right now, do something about it. Move heaven and earth if you must. Don't stop until you reach where you want to be.

Closing.

Knowing what's holding you back is the first step you need to take to overcome them. Acknowledge these blockers and work on them. If you are afraid to fail, remember that failure is just part of the whole journey. If you are afraid of the uncertainties, remember that all our choices are half chances. And if we are afraid that we might just be wasting time, remember that whatever the outcome that your learning and experiences will make all your effort worth it in the end. You are not defined by the amount of effort you put in, not your failures.

I hope this video inspires you to always choose to look at things positively and outgrow whatever hinders you. No matter what your circumstances are, you have the power to turn things around and succeed. Many people have done it and trust that you can also do it. If you like this video, please give it a thumbs up and subscribe for more.

PART 2

Chapter 1:

How to Determine What Makes You Happy

Finding your happiness is an art, not science, but here are five things I've done to help me figure where my happiness is coming from.

1. Wipe Your Happiness Slate Clean

If you're a human who is alive, the society you grew up in has Ideas about what happiness looks like. These ideas have permeated our lives since the moment we could understand shapes and colors; they've wormed their way into our soft, sweet subconsciouses.

On some level, most of us believe we will be happier when:

- We are thinner than we are now

- We earn more money

- We live in a bigger, prettier, better-located home

- We have more friends

- We're in a committed romantic relationship

And maybe some of those things really will make us happier! Supportive relationships and aerobic activity have been shown to reduce depression.

I imagine moving into a space with more natural light, and a shorter commute wouldn't hurt anything, either.

But for the sake of this experiment, let's do our very, very best to let go of preconceived notions about what makes us happy. Let's forget what our families and friends believe happiness looks like. Let's view this as a grand experiment with totally unknown results. Who knows what we'll discover!

P.S. Don't get down on yourself for "buying into cultural expectations of happiness." We all do it. We're not robots. For Pete's sake, Oprah's been trying to diet her way to happiness for two decades.

2. Start Taking Detailed Notes When You Feel Really Happy

Do you know those moments of "*If this isn't nice, I don't know what is*"? Those moments when you'd lift your face to the sky and grin (but you don't because it feels awkward), make a note of *those* moments. Open up the 'notes' app on your phone and type in what, exactly, you were doing.

Yes, I know this is dorky. And, yes, I know you're thinking, "I should do that!" And then you're not going to do it.

Do it. I think you'll be surprised by what makes you happy.

3. Remind yourself, "This makes me happy."

Many of the things that make me happy are, to be honest, a hassle (and by 'hassle,' I mean "require me to put on real clothes, google something, and leave the house"). Intellectually, I know taking a day trip to Hudson, working in a new coffee shop, and then hanging out on the sandbar will make me happy … but it is just SO MUCH EASIER to keep working at home in my yoga pants.

Here's how I remember what makes me happy:

- I wrote a list of the things that make me happy – big and little, easy and difficult – and posted that list next to my computer. Whenever my mind wanders, whenever I'm feeling blue, I can look to the right of my computer screen and remember that reading a chapter of <u>this</u> book while cuddling the dog will make me happy.

- When I'm in the middle of doing something that makes me happy, I say to myself, "This makes me happy."

Am I eating chocolate mousse at a supper club in rural South Dakota? *"This makes me happy."*

Am I hiking around a lake on a sunny Tuesday afternoon? *"This makes me happy."*

I just bought an amazing chair on Craigslist for $50? *"This makes me happy."*

Reciting this little phrase helps cement these happy-making habits in my brain and life. It helps me feel proud to take steps to have the life I want. It reminds me that the hassle of happiness – the planning, the boundary-pushing, the saving, and scheduling – is worth it.

Chapter 2:
6 Steps To Get Out of Your Comfort Zone

The year 2020 and 2021 have made a drastic change in all our lives, which might have its effect forever. The conditions of last year and a half have made a certain lifestyle choice for everyone, without having a say in it for us.

This new lifestyle has been a bit overwhelming for some and some started feeling lucky. Most of us feel comfortable working from home, and taking online classes while others want to have some access to public places like parks and restaurants.

But the pandemic has affected everyone more than once. And now we are all getting used to this relatively new experience of doing everything from home. Getting up every day to the same routine and the same environment sometimes takes us way back on our physical and mental development and creativity.

So one must learn to leave the comfort zone and keep themselves proactive. Here are some ways anyone can become more productive and efficient.

Everyone is always getting ready to change but never changing.

1. Remember your Teenage Self

People often feel nostalgic remembering those days of carelessness when they were kids and so oblivious in that teenage. But, little do they take for inspiration or motivation from those times. When you feel down, or when you don't feel like having the energy for something, just consider your teenage self at that time.

If only you were a teenager now, you won't be feeling lethargic or less motivated. Rather you'd be pushing harder and harder every second to get the job done as quickly as possible. If you could do it back then, you still can! All you need is some perspective and a medium to compare to.

2. Delegate or Mentor someone

Have you ever needed to have someone who could provide you some guidance or help with a problem that you have had for some time?

I'm sure, you weren't always a self-made man or a woman. Somewhere along the way, there was someone who gave you the golden quote that changed you consciously or subconsciously.

Now is the time for you to do the same for someone else. You could be a teacher, a speaker, or even a mentor who doesn't have any favors to ask in return. Once you get the real taste of soothing someone else's pain, you won't hesitate the next time.

This feeling of righteousness creates a chain reaction that always pushes you to get up and do good for anyone who could need you.

3. Volunteer in groups

The work of volunteering may seem pointless or philanthropic. But the purpose for you to do it should be the respect that you might get, but the stride to get up on your feet and help others to be better off.

Volunteering for flood victims, earthquake affectees or the starving people of deserts and alpines can help you understand the better purpose of your existence. This keeps the engine of life running.

4. Try New Things for a Change

Remember the time in Pre-school when your teachers got you to try drawing, singing, acting, sculpting, sketching, and costume parties. Those weren't some childish approach to keep you engaged, but a planned system to get your real talents and skills to come out.

We are never too old to learn something new. Our passions are unlimited just as our dreams are. We only need a push to keep discovering the new horizons of our creative selves.

New things lead to new people who lead to new places which might lead to new possibilities. This is the circle of life and life is ironic enough to rarely repeat the same thing again.

You never know which stone might lead you to a gold mine. So never stop discovering and experiencing because this is what makes us the supreme being.

5. Push Your Physical Limits

This may sound cliched, but it always is the most important point of them all. You can never get out of your comfort zone, till you see the world through the hard glass.

The world is always softer on one side, but the image on the other side is far from reality. You can't expect to get paid equally to the person who works 12 hours a day in a large office of hundreds of employees. Only if you have the luxury of being the boss of the office.

You must push yourself to search for opportunities at every corner. Life has always more and better to offer at each stop, you just have to choose a stop.

6. Face Your Fears Once and For All

People seem to have a list of Dos and Dont's. The latter part is mostly because of a fear or a vacant thought that it might lead to failure for several reasons.

You need a "Do it all" behavior in life to have an optimistic approach to everything that comes in your way.

What is the biggest most horrible thing that can happen if you do any one of these things on your list? You need to have a clear vision of the possible worst outcome.

If you have a clear image of what you might lose, now must try to go for that thing and remove your fear once and for all. Unless you have something as important as your life to lose, you have nothing to fear from anything.

No one can force you to directly go skydiving if you are scared of heights. But you can start with baby steps, and then, maybe, later on in life you dare to take a leap of faith.

"Life is a rainbow, you might like one color and hate the other. But that doesn't make it ugly, only less tempting".

All you need is to be patient and content with what you have today, here, right now. But, you should never stop aiming for more. And you certainly shouldn't regret it if you can't have or don't have it now.

People try to find their week spots and frown upon those moments of hard luck. What they don't realize is, that the time they wasted crying for what is in the past, could have been well spent for a far better future they could cherish for generations to come.

Chapter 3:

6 Concerning Effects of Mood On Your Life

By definition, mood is the predominant state of our mind which clouds over all the other emotions and judgements. Our mood represents the surface-level condition of our emotional self.

Mood is very versatile and sensitive. Subtle changes in our surroundings or even changes in our thoughts directly affect mood. And consequently, our mood, being the leader of our mental state, affects us, as a whole—even impacting our life directly.

Take notes of these following points so that you can overpower your mood and take complete control of your life.

Here Are 6 Ways How Changes In Your Mood Can Impact Your Life:

1. Mood On Your Judgement and Decision-Making

Humans are the most rational beings—fitted with the most advanced neural organ, the brain. Scientists say that our brain is capable of making one thousand trillion logical operations per second and yet still, we humans are never surprised to make the stupidest of judgements in real life.

Well, along with such an enormous 'Logical reasoning' capacity, our brains also come with an emotional center and that is where mood comes in to crash all logic. Most of the decisions we make are emotional, not logical. Since our emotions are steered by mood, it is no surprise that we often make irrational decisions out of emotional impulses.

But again, there are also some instances where mood-dictated decisions reap better outcomes compared to a logical decision. That's just life.

2. Mood Affects Your Mental Health

While our mood is a holistic reflection of our mental state caused by various external and internal factors, it is also a fact that our mood can be the outcome of some harboring mental illness. Both high degree of euphoria and depression can be an indication of mood disorder—just on two opposite ends of the spectrum.

There is no specific cause behind it except that it is a culmination of prolonged mood irregularities. And mood irregularities may come from anywhere i.e. worrying, quarrelling, drug abuse, period/puberty, hormonal changes etc. If such mood irregularity persists untreated, it may deteriorate your overall mental health and result in more serious conditions. So, consider monitoring your mood changes often.

3. Correlation Between Mood and Physical Well-Being

We have heard the proverb that goes, "A healthy body is a healthy mind". Basically, our body and mind function together. So, if your body is in a healthy state, your mind will reflect it by functioning properly as well. If on the other hand your body is not in a healthy state, due to lack of proper nutrition, sleep, and exercise, then your mind will become weak as well. Yes, according to research, having a persistent bad mood can lead to chronic stress which gradually creates hormonal imbalance in your body and thus, diseases like diabetes, hypertension, stroke etc. may arise in your body. Negative moods can also make you go age faster than usual. So having a cheerful mood not only keeps you happy but also fuels your body and keeps you young. Aim to keep your body in tip top condition to nourish the mind as well.

4. Effect Of Your Mood On Others

This is obvious, right? You wouldn't smile back at your significant other after you have lost your wallet, spilled hot coffee all over yourself and missed the only bus to your job interview.

Your mood overshadows how you behave with others. The only way to break out of this would be to meditate and achieve control over your emotional volatility—believe that whatever happened, happened for a reason. Your sully mood doesn't warrant being hostile with others. Instead, talk to people who want the best of you. Express your griefs.

5. Mood As A Catalyst In Your Productivity

Tech giants like Google, Apple, Microsoft all have certain 'play areas' for the employees to go and play different games. It is there to remove mental stress of the employees because mood is an essential factor in determining your productivity at work-place. According to experts, people with a negative mood are 10% less productive in their work than those who are in a positive mood. This correlation between mood and productivity is an important thing to be concerned about.

6. Mood Change Your Perspective

Everyone has their own point of view. Perspectives of people vary from individual to individual and similarly, it varies depending on the mood of an individual. On a bad day, even your favorite Starbucks drink would feel tasteless. It doesn't mean that they made a bad drink—it means that you're not in the mood of enjoying its taste. So, how you perceive things and people is greatly affected by your mindset. Pro-tip: Don't throw judgement over someone or something carrying a bad mood. You'll regret it later and think "I totally misread this".

Final Thoughts

Our mood has plenty of implications on our life. Though our mood is an external representation of our overall mental state, it has its effect on very miniscule aspects of our life to large and macroscopic levels. In the long run, our mood alone can be held responsible for what we have done our whole life—the choices we've made. Though it is really difficult to control our mood, we can always try. Meditating may be one of the possible ways to have our mood on the noose. Because no matter what happens, you wouldn't want your whole life to be an outcome of your emotional impulses would you?

Chapter 4:

How to Acknowledge The Unhappy Moments?

In today's video we will talk about how we can embrace the unhappiness moments in our lives and turn them into power and strength that will carry us through life gracefully.

We all have moments in life when we are not happy, we're scared, we're apprehensive, mildly depressed even, and the pain is difficult to endure. Whether it be because we have lost a friend, someone we love, or that we are simply not happy at our jobs. There could be a million reasons for our unhappiness.

In these trying times we only want an escape. To escape from our pain, our unhappy feelings because we are not ready to deal with the things that are going wrong in our lives. We don't want to acknowledge our unhappy moments because this makes us grieve and inflict more pain.

All these ways of avoiding the acknowledgment only perpetuate our feelings in long run. Avoidance only brings us misery and suffering in the long run. It keeps us from living to our fullest potential. It keeps us from the very fact that there is light at the end of the tunnel, and that we need to keep moving forward.

It is very important that you acknowledge your unhappy moments because you can only move forward with confidence once you accept that life being unhappy is simply a part of life. How can you admire happiness and the joys in your life if you have not gone through any unhappy moments? If you have nothing to compare it to?

It is not always easy to acknowledge the unhappy moments in life. But here are 5 powerful ways to help you along with the process.

Recognize the Reason of your unhappiness

First step of acknowledgment is to recognize the problem, find the real reason why you are unhappy. If, for example, you think you are not happy at your job, instead of pointing fingers at the obvious issues you are facing, ask yourself the deeper questions. Questions like, do I feel like I belong here? Do I feel I'm making a difference? Is what I am doing fulfilling my true desires? If the answer to those questions is a resounding no, it could be that your heart is, at that very moment, not in this job. You might be feeling as though you are spinning on a hamster wheel, going around in circles with nowhere in sight. It is very important to understand the true reason for your unhappiness because you cannot cut the stem and think that the tree will not grow again.

Take a moment and stop

Once you have found the problem, take a moment, and just stop right there. Don't suppress the feelings. Take a deep breath and sit with it for a while. Just sit there and be with it. Acknowledge that you have identified the essence of the unhappiness that had been festering in you for a while. And be glad that you now have something to work with to change your situation.

Accept what it is

Once you have found the root of the problem it's time to accept it. As Thick Nhat mentioned in his book "Peace is every step". He writes that it is important to mentally acknowledge our feelings. Say out loud if you feel like it, "I can accept that I am experiencing intense unhappiness right now. And that it is okay. And that I will be okay."

Once you have embraced your moments of unhappiness you can overcome the feelings and move forward with peace.

If you are embracing your moments of unhappiness, you can create a mental space and see around it instead of being enmeshed in them. This space will open new doors and help you overcome your feelings as you embrace new beginnings that will soon come your way.

Plan Next Best Move

Now that you have successfully identified the reason for your unhappiness, it is time to find out what your next best move is. In life we never really know what the next right move is, we can only hope and trust that our decisions will work for us in the end.

Take the time to write down the things you want and the things that can change your situation. Things that can potentially move you out from a place of unhappiness. Going back to the previous problem that we have discussed, if it is your job that is causing distress in your life, what are the potential ways you can apply to mitigate the problem, would it be to quit or could you find a compromise somewhere. Talking to a colleague, a friend, or even your boss to let you explore your areas of creativity and things you excel at could be a welcome change.

Whatever the potential may be, no matter how big or small, you have the power to change your situation. Don't stay trapped in that situation for too long as it will only bring you down further along the road.

Believe Things Will Work Out In The End

Hope is a very powerful thing. Now that we have a plan, we need to have faith and just believe that our actions will pay off. We can never predict the future, and so taking one step at a time is the best thing we can do. We have to believe that whatever we are doing to change our situation will turn our unhappiness around sooner or later.

Final Thoughts

Happy and unhappy moments are part of life, like day and night, light, and darkness.

If you only believe in one thing, believe that change is the only constant and that bad times don't last forever. You will be happy again and you will move forward gracefully. And this is only possible if acknowledge your unhappy moments.

Happiness Is just right around the corner.

Chapter 5:

Becoming High Achievers

By becoming high achievers we become high off life, what better feeling is there than aiming for something you thought was unrealistic and then actually hitting that goal.

What better feeling is there than declaring we will do something against the perceived odds and then actually doing it.

To be a high achiever you must be a believer,

You must believe in yourself and believe that dream is possible for you.

It doesn't matter what anyone else thinks , as long as you believe,

To be a high achiever we must hunger to achieve.

To be an action taker.

Moving forward no matter what.

High achievers do not quit.

Keeping that vision in their minds eye until it becomes reality, no matter what.

Your biggest dream is protected by fear , loss and pain.

We must conquer all 3 of these impostors to walk through the door.

Not many do , most are still fighting fear and if they lose the battle, they quit.

Loss and pain are part of life.

Losses are hard on all of us.

Whether we lose possessions, whether we lose friends, whether we lose our jobs, or whether we lose family members.

Losing doesn't mean you have lost.

Losses are may be a tough pill to swallow, but they are essential because we cannot truly succeed until we fail.

We can't have the perfect relationship if we stay in a toxic one, and we can't have the life we desire until we make room by letting go of the old.

The 3 imposters that cause us so much terror are actually the first signs of our success. So walk through fear in courage , look at loss as an eventual gain, and know that the pain is part of the game and without it you would be weak.

Becoming a high achiever requires a single minded focus on your goal, full commitment and an unnatural amount of persistence and work.

We must define what high achievement means to us individually, set the bar high and accept nothing less.

The achievement should not be money as money is not our currency but a tool.

The real currency is time and your result is the time you get to experience the world's places and products , so the result should always be that.

The holiday home , the fast car and the lifestyle of being healthy and wealthy, those are merely motivations to work towards. Like Carrots on a stick.

High achievement is individual to all of us, it means different things to each of us,

But if we are going to go for it we might as well go all out for the life we want, should we not?

I don't think we beat the odds of 1 in 400 trillion to be born, just to settle for mediocrity, did we?

Being a high achiever is in your DNA , if you can beat the odds , you can beat anything.

It is all about self-belief and confidence, we must have the confidence to take the action required and often the risk.

Risk is difficult for people and it's a difficult tight rope to walk. The line between risk and recklessness is razor thin.

Taking risks feels unnatural, not surprisingly as we all grew up in a health and safety bubble with all advice pointing towards safe and secure ways.

But the reward is often in the risk and sometimes a leap of blind faith is required. This is what stops most of us - the fear of the unknown.

The truth is the path to success is foggy and we can only ever see one step ahead , we have to imagine the result and know it's somewhere down this foggy path and keep moving forward with our new life in mind.

Know that we can make it but be aware that along the path we will be met by fear , loss and pain and the bigger our goal the bigger these monsters will be.

The top achievers financially are fanatical about their work and often work 100+ hours per week.

Some often work day and night until a project is successful.

Being a high achiever requires giving more than what is expected, standing out for the high standard of your work because being known as number 1 in your field will pay you abundantly.

Being an innovator, thinking outside the box for better practices, creating superior products to your competition because quality is more rewarding than quantity.

Maximizing the quality of your products and services to give assurance to your customers that your company is the number 1 choice.

What can we do differently to bring a better result to the table and a better experience for our customers?

We must think about questions like that because change is inevitable and without thinking like that we get left behind, but if we keep asking that, we can successfully ride the wave of change straight to the beach of our desired results.

The route to your success is by making people happy because none of us can do anything alone, we must earn the money and to earn it we must make either our employers or employees and customers happy.

To engage in self-promotion and positive interaction with those around us, we must be polite and positive with everyone, even with our competition.

Because really the only competition is ourselves and that is all we should focus on.

Self-mastery, how can I do better than yesterday?

What can I do different today that will improve my circumstances for tomorrow.

Little changes add up to a big one.

The belief and persistence towards your desired results should be 100%, I will carry on until… is the right attitude.

We must declare to ourselves that we will do this , we don't yet know how but we know that we will.

Because high achievers like yourselves know that to make it you must endure and persist untill you win.

High achievers have an unnatural grit and thick skin , often doing what others won't, putting in the extra hours when others don't.

After you endure loss and conquer pain , the sky is the limit, and high achievers never settle until they are finished.

Chapter 6:

10 Habits to Start Right Now

Have you ever wondered why you are not able to achieve your goals and aspirations? You might get a little confused while searching for the stumbling block on the way to your success, but the answer is simple and right in front of you. It is procrastination and some other unhealthy habits.

Here are ten healthy habits that you need to start incorporating in your life immediately.

1. Maintaining a Routine

You can't expect that everything will be in order one fine morning and you will start achieving all your goals suddenly just like that. It doesn't work that way. Success comes when you start taking small steps every day and slowly work on your progress little by little. You need to start to maintain a routine regularly. Doing this will help you get rid of your procrastination. You can start with simple things like doing some household chores like cooking, cleaning, etc. Let's say you have decided to cook every day – whenever you think that you need to cook all three meals and for everyone, it might intimidate you. You can start with small tasks that are more manageable. So, start with cooking an item every day. That won't take much time and won't be that difficult either – once you start doing this, start increasing the amount and intensity of the work. After you understand how this routine thing works, you can slowly move towards the work related to your goals and aspirations and maintain a routine.

2. Embracing Immediacy

Most people like to put things aside for doing those later. It is a huge mistake that can have serious consequences. People procrastinate everything like problematic things, easy things, small things, big things, and fun things. When you put aside something for doing it later, it gets more challenging to do with time. So, you just keep pushing it further and further until there is no time left to do it. You can overcome this by immediacy. Whenever you are reminded or informed about some work, start doing it immediately and don't keep it pending for later. If it is a small thing that requires a little time to finish, then make sure to finish it in one go. If it is a long work, start working immediately and take breaks and work whenever possible.

3. React Thoughtfully

Most people allow their emotions to control their reactions. Try to avoid making decisions while your emotions are heightened. This is because the decisions that are taken while emotions are heightened are usually wrong decisions and can have detrimental consequences. Your heightened emotions make you blind, and you do things that you wouldn't have done otherwise. So, whenever something triggers you, don't let your gut reaction out. Wait for some time, probably 5-6 minutes, and then act. When you give yourself a little time, it allows you to see through the situation and think beyond those overwhelming emotions. It will make you see the bigger picture and react thoughtfully.

4. Quitting Clicks, Swipes, and Scrolls

Do you even realize how much time you spend aimlessly clicking, swiping, or scrolling? It wastes a lot of your time and is also responsible for draining your productivity, concentration, and motivation. A little bit of digital media does no harm. It is, in fact, helpful because you can get loads of information from the media. But if you keep scrolling for hours, that is where the problem begins. You need to cut down on your use of media to allow yourself to get benefitted from it. If you find difficulty reducing the use of media by yourself, you can try using a browser blocker. It will block all the media outlets after a specified amount of time, thereby limiting the time you spend over there.

5. Embracing the Old

It is usual for people to crave new things every time. But sometimes, people get so overwhelmed by the excitement of trying to gain something new that they forget to cherish the things they already have in their possession. Gaining something you wanted to can be a little exciting and fun for some time, but this will just feed your urge to gain more and more things. Most people already possess everything they require, but they don't seem to see it because of the urge to get something new. For example, a person having a closet full of clothes keeps on buying new clothes every time he has somewhere to go. If you find yourself in a similar situation, you can avoid this by looking at the closet carefully and observing everything you have in your possession. You can, maybe, rearrange the closet in a way where you will be able to see stuff the way you want to see. Once you start cherishing the things that you already have, you can go a long way.

6. Remember Your Achievements

Sometimes, you are too harsh on yourself, and you blame yourself way too much. You should always treat yourself with the same amount of kindness and positivity you possess while treating others. Everyone has their fair share of successes and failures in their lives. So, you should be grateful for everything you achieved and not take those for granted. Instead of regretting and blaming yourself for the things you couldn't achieve, try reminding yourself amount the things you actually did achieve. Appreciate yourself for every good thing that you have done in your life. It can be something like quitting certain habits, scoring certain marks in an exam, doing something good for others, etc. So, whenever you make some mistake, you need to remind yourself of all the small and big things you have achieved so that you don't get too disheartened to get up and move on. Embrace the good in you!

7. Declutter

Have you ever felt that whenever you change the orientation of the furniture in your room, you get excited and feel different? This is because even a tiny change is considered to be new, fun, and exciting. Your motivation and productivity get hugely affected by your workspace environment. If your workspace environment is messy, it is going to inspire your creativity subconsciously. In contrast, if you have a well-organized workspace, it will subconsciously boost your efficiency and help you remove any mental clutter. Keep changing your workspace from time to time. Keep it messy somedays, for increasing your creativity levels. When you need to do a lot of hard work that demands efficiency, arrange everything in order and make your workspace well-organized. You can add some photo frames to give it a different and exciting look.

8. Set Small Achievable Goals Everyday

People feel the most satisfied when they know that they have achieved a certain goal. You can use it to your advantage for brightening up your day. Set small achievable goals throughout your day so that you can easily achieve them. It can be as simple as making your bed after you get up, and so on. Make sure that you already have 2-3 achieved goals before you have your breakfast. These small benchmarks play a vital role in kick-starting your day on a good note. All these little benchmarks add up and give you a sense of pride and satisfaction after you achieve them, thereby brightening up your day.

9. Give Compliments

People love to receive compliments from others but get a little shaky while giving compliments to others. Have you ever wondered why? It is probably because you worry about how it would make you look like. You feel that complimenting others can make you look lighter and easy. That's absolutely not the case. Complimenting people can really help you start a conversation with different people and get friendly. It is a fantastic social skill that you need to learn because of the various benefits it offers. Don't fear what others will think, and don't sugarcoat your words either. Because when you give fake compliments, people can feel that it is not coming from your heart, leaving a very negative impression on them. Try to be as genuine as possible and speak your mind out.

10. Commit to Relaxation

A lot of people work continuously, and even when they are taking a break, all they think about is their work! It is not a healthy habit and needs to be changed immediately. When you work yourself too much and don't give yourself the amount of relaxation it deserves, work seems to be more complicated than it actually is, thereby reducing your productivity and concentration. When you feel like you can't work anymore and that you have reached your threshold cut yourself some slack! When you are taking a break, make sure not to think about work at all. Plan something relaxing, exciting, or fun, and enjoy yourself fully while taking some time off from your work. It will recharge your mind, and then you can return to your work, being energetic and positive.

I hope you follow these steps and develop them as habits in your daily life so that you can make the most out of your life and stay happy.

Chapter 7:

6 Ways To Get People To Like You

We are always trying for people to like us. We work on ourselves so that we can impress them. Everyone can not enjoy a single person. There will always be someone who dislikes them. But, that one person does not stop us from being charming and making people like us. In today's generation, good people are difficult to find. We all have our definition of being liked. We all have our type of person to select. That makes it very hard for someone to like someone by just knowing their name. We always judge people quickly, even to understand their nature. That makes it hard to like someone.

People always work their selves to be liked by the majority of people. It gives you a sense of comfort knowing that people are happy with you. You feel at ease when you know that people around you tend to smile by thinking about you. For that, you need to make an excellent first impression on people. Training yourself in such a way that you become everyone's favorite can sure be tiring. But, it always comes with a plus point.

1. **Don't Judge**

If you want people to like you, then you need to stop judging them. It is not good to consider someone based on rumors or by listening to one side of the story. Don't judge at all. We can never have an idea of what's going on in an individual life. We can not know what they are going through without them telling us. The best we can do is not judge them. Give them time to open up. Let them speak with you without the fear of being judged. Assuming someone is the worst without you them knowing is a horrendous thing to do.

2. Let Go of Your Ego and Arrogance

Make people feel like they can talk to you anytime they want. Arrogance will lead you nowhere. You will only be left alone in the end. So, make friends. Don't be picky about people. Try to get to know everyone with their own stories and theories. Make them feel comfortable around you to willingly come to talk to you and feel at ease after a few words with you. Being egotistic may make people fear you, but it will not make people like you. Be friendly with everyone around you.

3. Show Your Interest In People

When people talk about their lives, let them. Be interested in their lives, so it will make them feel unique around you. Make sure you listen attentively to their rant and remember as much as possible about a person. Even if they talk about something boring, try to make an effort towards them. If they talk about something worth knowledge, appreciate them. Ask them questions about it, or share your part of information with them, if you have any on that subject. Just try to make an effort, and people will like you instantly.

4. Try To Make New Friends

People admire others when they can click with anyone they meet. Making new friends can be a challenge, but it gives you confidence and, of course, new friends. Try to provide an excellent first impression and show them your best traits. Try to be yourself as much as possible, but do not go deep into friendship instantly. Give them time to adapt to your presence. You will notice that they will come to you themselves. That is because they like being around you. They trust you with their time, and you should valve it.

5. Be Positive

Everyone loves people. You give a bright, positive vibe. They tend to go to them, talk to them and listen to them. People who provide positive energy are easy to communicate with, and we can almost instantly become friends. Those are the type of people we can trust and enjoy being around. Positivity plays a critical role in your want to be liked. It may not be easy, but practice makes perfect. You have to give it your all and make everyone happy.

6. Be Physically and Mentally Present For The People Who Need You

People sometimes need support from their most trusted companion. You have to make sure you are there for them whenever they need you. Be there for them physically, and you can comfort someone without even speaking with them. Just hug them or just try to be there for them. It will make them feel peaceful by your presence. Or be there emotionally if they are ready. Try to talk to them. Listen to whatever they have to say, even if it doesn't make sense. And if they need comfort. Try to motivate them with your words.

Conclusion

You need to improve yourself immensely if you want people to like you. Make sure you do the right thing at the right time. Make people trust you and make them believe your words. Even a small gesture can make people like you. Have the courage to change yourself so that people will like you with all their heart's content.

Chapter 8:

8 Habits That Help You Live Longer

Habits define who you are. Each habit influences your life on a positive and negative dimensions. After all, smoking a cigarette is a habit, and so are long hours of jogging. The behaviors that negative you from attaining your full potential also shorten your life.

Exercising, consuming nutritious meals, meditating, among others, makes our lives better in immeasurable ways. Our habits take over as an autopilot when our physical and mental abilities ebb and flow with age. This is especially true if you are old enough to understand the importance of habits but still young enough to make your positive habits count. As you get older, you'll find yourself relying more and more on your habits. Create good habits, and they will serve as the autopilot on which you will trust to stay healthy, active, and engaged.

As you create and stick to that habit you love, keep longevity and quality life your ultimate goal. Even if you've had bad habits in the past, now is the moment to break them.

Here are 8 habits that could help you live a longer life.

1. Exercise Regularly.

Studies show that frequent, intense exercising is essential for age and physical health preservation. Getting out of your comfort zone to engage in a challenging exercise will reap benefits in the long haul. Hopping on a treadmill at a snail-like pace will do you no good. Therefore, it would help if you stalled rigorous aerobic exercises, stretching to your habit menu.

The less flexible you are, the more likely you will trip, break your hip, and end up in a nursing home like Aunt Karen. Vigorous exercise and stretching your body are the best ways to protect yourself from preventable injuries and the physical ailments of aging.

2. Mind Training

Mind training is equally vital as body exercises as you become older. As you train your body, your mind also needs activity to stay in good form. Learn and challenge yourself to remain alert and possibly avoid dementia. There are many mind training exercises such as puzzles, or even Sudoku, or any mind-challenging tasks.

According to a recent study conducted by John Hopkins Medicine, staying in school longer reduces the prevalence of dementia in the United States, particularly among individuals aged 65 and older.

3. Keep a Healthy Weight.

Maintaining a healthy body means that you are cautious of what you consume. Consider the foods that enhance your physical, mental and spiritual wellbeing by avoiding calories and refined food staff. A new article in Medical News Today by Catharine Paddock, Ph.D., advocates keeping your body mass index (BMI) under 25% if possible. Keep your body weight as healthy as possible! It will impact your longevity.

4. Develop a Positive Mental Attitude.

Whatever your viewpoint is on your present living conditions, impact your life in the long haul. That is, your take on your current life significantly reacts with the functioning of your body and soul. Therefore, people who adopt and adjust to a positive stereotype about aging are likely to recover faster from any disability. As a result, according to a recent study published in the Journal of the American Medical Association, longevity is achieved by maintaining positive thoughts towards your current state of affairs.

5. Elevate Your Mood.

As we become older, depression and anxiety might become more prevalent. Do anything you can to boost your mood, whether it's through exercise or exciting mental activity. Go for walks in the park, re-enter the dating scene, or volunteer for a cause you care about – in short, do anything that makes you feel better about yourself and the world.

6. Maintain Your Social Contacts.

Maintaining a social connection becomes meaningful as you grow older. You don't need a considerable social network; an influential network is enough. Your family, accordingly, may be enough, but only if the members are happy and flourishing. The Inverse is very true! If you find that your social network is exceptionally negative, look for ways to create a new one.

Make friends of different ages who may have other interests than you, and keep fostering friendships you already have or may have had in the past. Remember, that person you allow in your inner circle is equally important.

7. Take Charge of Your Life

Rather than being a spectator, own your life. Don't just sit and watch the world pass you. Just get out and about, engage in activities that matter at every stage of your life. This means doing what a 25 or 40-year-old does to avoid mid-life crises. It can be not easy, especially in today's internet era, where we can check what other people are up to at the hour without even leaving the couch. On the other hand, sitting on the sidelines will not help you maintain excellent physical or mental health. Make sure you're not only listening to other people's experiences; get out there and make your own.

8. Do Something Valuable.

Having a purpose in life and living up to it is vital. The drive doesn't have to be extravagant or mid-blowing to be meaningful as most of us think. Some people find their purpose in being an outstanding grandparent, volunteering for a cause important to them, or even mastering woodworking or gardening skills. It doesn't matter what your goal is as long as you have one.

On the other hand, not having a purpose might lead to poor habits that negatively impact your longevity and mood. Consider this: if you don't have anything to do, you can end up sitting in front of the TV all day, or worse, falling into the meaningless emptiness of social media.

Conclusion

The great news is that you don't have to take multi-vitamins or pharmaceuticals-promoted drugs to halt aging, hunger yourself, and thirst to reduce weight, or buy the latest products promising increased brain performance. According to several studies, adopting basic steps in the short term can result in longevity benefits.

Chapter 9:

Do More of What Already Works

In 2004, nine hospitals in Michigan began implementing a new procedure in their intensive care units (I.C.U.). Almost overnight, healthcare professionals were stunned by its success.

Three months after it began, the procedure had cut the infection rate of I.C.U. Patients by sixty-six percent. Within 18 months, this one method had saved 75 million dollars in healthcare expenses. Best of all, this single intervention saved the lives of more than 1,500 people in just a year and a half. The strategy was immediately published in a blockbuster paper for the <u>New England Journal of Medicine</u>.

This medical miracle was also simpler than you could ever imagine. It was a checklist.

This five-step checklist was the simple solution that Michigan hospitals used to save 1,500 lives. Think about that for a moment. There were no technical innovations. There were no pharmaceutical discoveries or cutting-edge procedures. The physicians just stopped skipping steps. They implemented the answers they already had on a more consistent basis.

New Solutions vs. Old Solutions

We tend to undervalue answers that we have already discovered. We underutilize old solutions—even best practices—because they seem like something we have already considered.

Here's the problem: *"Everybody already knows that"* is very different from *"Everybody already does that."* Just because a solution is known doesn't mean it is utilized.

Even more critical, just because a solution is implemented occasionally doesn't mean it is implemented consistently. Every physician knew the five steps on Peter Pronovost's checklist, but very few did all five steps flawlessly each time.

We assume that new solutions are needed to make real progress, but that isn't always the case. This pattern is just as present in our personal lives as it is in corporations and governments. We waste the resources and ideas at our fingertips because they don't seem new and exciting.

There are many examples of behaviors, big and small, that have the opportunity to drive progress in our lives if we just did them with more consistency—flossing every day—never missing workouts. Performing fundamental business tasks each day, not just when you have time—apologizing more often. Writing Thank You notes each week.

Of course, these answers are boring. Mastering the fundamentals isn't sexy, but it works. No matter what task you are working on, a simple checklist of steps you can follow right now—fundamentals that you have known about for years—can immediately yield results if you just practice them more consistently.

Progress often hides behind boring solutions and underused insights. You don't need more information. You don't need a better strategy. You just need to do more of what already works.

Chapter 10:

Deal With Your Fears Now

Fear is a strange thing.

Most of our fears are phantoms that never actually appear or become real,

Yet it holds such power over us that it stops us from making steps forward in our lives.

It is important to deal with fear as it not only holds you back but also keeps you caged in irrational limitations.

Your life is formed by what you think.

It is important not to dwell or worry about anything negative.

Don't sweat the small stuff, and it's all small stuff (Richard Carlson).

It's a good attitude to have when avoiding fear.

Fear can be used as a motivator for yourself.

If you're in your 30s, you will be in your 80s in 50 years, then it will be too late.

And that doesn't mean you will even have 50 years. Anything could happen.

But let's say you do, that's 50 years to make it and enjoy it.

But to enjoy it while you are still likely to be healthy, you have a maximum of 15 years to make it - minus sleep and living you are down to 3 years.

If however you are in your 40s, you better get a move on quickly.

Does that fear not dwarf any possible fears you may have about taking action now?

Dealing with other fears becomes easy when the ticking clock is staring you in the face.

Most other fears are often irrational.

We are only born with two fears, the fear of falling and the fear of load noises.

The rest have been forced on us by environment or made up in our own minds.

The biggest percentage of fear never actually happens.

To overcome fear we must stare it in the face and walk through it knowing our success is at the other side.
Fear is a dream killer and often stops people from even trying.
Whenever you feel fear and think of quitting, imagine behind you is the ultimate fear of the clock ticking away your life.

If you stop you lose and the clock is a bigger monster than any fear.
If you let anything stop you the clock will catch you.

So stop letting these small phantoms prevent you from living,
They are stealing your seconds, minutes, hours , days and weeks.
If you carry on being scared, they will take your months, years and decades.
Before you know it they have stolen your life.

You are stronger than fear but you must display true strength that fear will be scared.
It will retreat from your path forever if you move in force towards it because fear is fear and by definition is scared.

We as humans are the scariest monsters on planet Earth.
So we should have nothing to fear
Fear tries to stop us from doing our life's work and that is unacceptable.
We must view life's fears as the imposters they are, mere illusions in our mind trying to control us.

We are in control here.
We have the free will to do it anyway despite fear.
Take control and fear will wither and disappear as if it was never here.
The control was always yours you just let fear steer you off your path.

Fear of failure, fear of success, fear of what people will think.

All irrational illusions.

All that matters is what you believe.

If your belief and faith in yourself is strong , fear will be no match for your will.

Les Brown describes fear as false evidence appearing real.

I've never seen a description so accurate.

Whenever fear rears its ugly head, just say to yourself this is false evidence appearing real.

Overcoming fear takes courage and strength in one's self.

We must develop more persistence than the resistance we will face when pursuing our dreams.

If we do not develop a thick skin and unwavering persistence we will be beaten by fear, loss and pain.

Our why must be so important that these imposters become small in comparison.

Because after all the life we want to live does dwarf any fears or set back that might be on the path.

Fear is insignificant.

Fear is just one thing of many we must beat into the ground to prove our worth.

Just another test that we must pass to gain our success.

Because success isn't your right,

You must fight

With all your grit and might

Make it through the night and shine your massive light on the world.

And show everyone you are a star.

PART 3

Chapter 1:

Creating Successful Habits

Successful people have successful habits.

If you're stuck in life, feeling like you're not going anywhere, take a hard look at your habits.

Success is built from our small daily habits accumulated together,

Without these building blocks, you will not get far in life.

Precise time management, attention to detail, these are the traits of all who have made it big.

To change your life, you must literally change your life, the physical actions and the mindset.

Just as with success, the same goes with health.

Do you have the habit of a healthy diet and regular athletic exercises?

Healthy people have healthy habits.

If you are unhappy about your weight and figure, point the finger at your habits once again.

To become healthy, happy and wealthy, we must first become that person in the mind.

Success is all psychological.

Success has nothing to do with circumstances.

Until we have mastered the habits of our thinking we cannot project this success on the world.

We must first decide clearly who we want to be.

We must decide what our values are.

We must decide what we want to achieve.

Then we must discipline ourselves to take control of our destiny.

Once we know who we are and what we want to do,
Behaving as if it were reality becomes easy.

We must start acting the part.
That is the measure of true faith.
We must act as if we have already succeeded.
As the old saying goes: "fake it UNTIL YOU MAKE IT"

Commit yourself with unwavering faith.
Commit yourself with careful and calculated action.
You will learn the rest along the way

Every habit works towards your success or failure,
No matter how big or how small.
The more you change your approach as you fail, the better your odds become.
Your future life will be the result of your actions today.
It will be positive or negative depending on your actions now.

You will attain free-will over your thoughts and actions.
The more you take control, the happier you will be.

Guard your mind from negativity.
Your mind is your sanctuary.
Ignore the scaremongering.
Treat your mind to pure motivation.

We cannot avoid problems.
Problems are a part of life.
Take control of the situation when it arises.
Have a habit of responding with action rather than fear.

Make a habit of noticing everybody and respecting everybody.

Build positive relationships and discover new ideas.

Be strong and courageous, yet gentle and reasonable.

These are the habits of successful leaders.

Be meticulous.

Be precise.

Be focused.

Make your bed in the morning.

Follow the path of drill sergeants in the royal marines and US navy seals.

Simple yet effective,

This one habit will shift your mindset first thing as you greet the new day.

Choose to meditate.

Find a comfortable place to get in touch with your inner-self.

Make it a habit to give yourself clarity of the mind and spirit.

Visualize your goals and make them a reality in your mind.

Choose to work in a state of flow.

Be full immersed in your work rather than be distracted.

To be productive we need to have an incredible habit of staying focused.

It will pay off.

It will pay dividends.

The results will be phenomenal.

Every single thing you choose to make a habit will add up.

No matter how big or how small,

Choose wisely.

Choose the habit of treating others with respect.

Treat the cleaner the same as you would with investors and directors.

Treat the poor the same as you would with the CEO of a multi-national company.

Our habits and attitude towards ourselves and others makes up our character.

Choose a habit of co-operation over competition,

After all the only true competition is with ourselves.

It doesn't matter whether someone is doing better than us as long as we are getting better.

If someone is doing better we should learn from them.

Make it a habit of putting ourselves into someone else's shoes.

We might stand to learn a thing or two.

No habit is too big or too small.

To be happy and successful we must do our best in them all.

Chapter 2:

10 Habits That Damage Your Brain

Our brain is the most vital and unrivaled organ in the body. I am talking about the 100 billion-plus brain cells that are responsible for controlling everything that our body does. But, what I find odd is that often, we tend to neglect our brain health over other parts of our body. We work out and are constantly taking care of our body yet we forget about the most important organ that is basically keeping us alive! Most people are seemingly unaware that our brain requires training and exercise too. I bet most of you already know how crucial habits are in shaping you and your life but did you know that some habits even kill your brain cells? What if I told you that you could be damaging your own brain? Yes. You heard me right. We engage in certain habits in our day-to-day lives that are seemingly harmless but have are damaging our brains. Some of these damages that our brain suffers are known to be long-term and even fatal in some cases. Some examples of brain damage are Dementia and Alzheimer's.

If you want to know what these habits are that you might be engaging in, I am going to discuss ten such habits that are damaging your brain without even you noticing that you should immediately remove them from your life.

1. Skipping Breakfast

How frequently do you skip breakfast? Well, most people skip breakfast due to an ongoing diet, to save time, some do not feel hungry in the morning or just because they do not think it is important enough. However, did you know that skipping breakfast actually leads to brain damage? Remember that our body has gone without any food for approximately 8 hours. When we sleep, our body uses the stored-up nutrients. So, therefore, you should always remember to replenish these nutrients so that the brain and the body have enough energy to function properly throughout the day. Similarly, another Japanese study of 80,000 subjects conducted in a period of over 15 years showed that people who skipped breakfast frequently suffered from a stroke and low blood pressure, which is very harmful to the brain. Did you know that not having breakfast lowers the blood glucose level of the brain? So, the next time you decide to pass on your breakfast, think about the damage you are causing to your own brain.

2. Consuming Too Much Sugar

How often do you crave for and indulge in candies and sugary drinks? Well, because another reason that leads to brain damage is when you consume too much sugar. I bet you already know how eating too much sweet stuff can affect your body health drastically, giving you diabetes and obesity. You might be planning to cut off your sugar intake to have that perfect waistline, but another very important reason why you might want to do so is to protect your brain from being undeveloped. Yes, too much sugar hinders your brain's capacity to develop. It is because when you consume a lot of candies and sweets, it disrupts your body's ability to absorb the important nutrients and proteins, which then results in your body not being able to send these to your brain. This makes your brain malnutritioned and stops its development.

3. Smoking

Smoking is probably the most harmful habit that a person might have. All of us already know smoking gives us a ton of diseases related to the heart and lungs, and not to forget cancer. Well, another reason why you should quit smoking starting today is that it brings about a ton of brain-related illnesses too. Did you know that smoking damages your brain membrane and neural viability of your brain that is responsible for balance, coordination, and motor skills? Not only that, smoking thins the cortex of your brain that deals with language, memory, and perception. Smoking is also a major cause of Dementia, Alzheimer's, and even death. It also leads to inflammation of the brain resulting in illnesses such as Multiple Sclerosis. Considering all this information, I would suggest you take quitting smoking more seriously.

4. Not Getting Enough Sleep

Did you know that sleep is crucial for both our physical and mental health? So, do you sleep enough? Or too much? The number of hours that you sleep has a direct impact on the functioning of your brain. Sleep deprivation is one of the most common things of this generation. But do you know that it can cause your brain to shrink its size? It can lead to serious issues such as depression, extreme daytime drowsiness, impaired memory. Studies have shown that it is only during the deep sleep cycle that the toxins in your brain are released. Even one night of sleep deprivations leads to issues such as not being able to recall new information and dysfunctioning of your brain. You are basically killing your brain cells by not improving your sleeping habits that will result in memory loss.

5. Covering Your Head When Sleeping

What if I told you that the way you sleep is also known to cause brain damage? You might be wondering how. But if you are among the many that cover their heads while they sleep, you are causing your brain damage. This is because it leads to carbon dioxide buildup as you will be intaking more carbon dioxide than oxygen to your brain. This can even cause you to have Dementia at an early age.

6. Blasting Music on Your Headphone

While listening to music on your headphones may be convenient, did you know that listening to loud music and not giving your ears a break causes you brain damage? If you are one of those who constantly listen to music, then you should probably give it a little more thought because you are damaging not only your ears but also your brain. Medical experts say that this can lead to hearing problems and also memory loss. Hearing problems are mostly related to brain problems such as loss of brain tissue. So, it is time you adjust your volume and gives your ears a break so that you can preserve your hearing and protect your brain from further damage.

7. Not Drinking Enough Water

Do you have a habit of over-looking your water intake? Because let me tell you that your brain needs an adequate amount of water to function properly, think faster, and focus better. It is no news that our body made up of 70% of water, right? Therefore, water is crucial to the body and the brain. Researchers say that dehydration has immediate effects on the brain. Even 2 hours of a heavy task without proper hydration can lead to disruptive cognitive functions. The brain needs sufficient water to clean out the toxins in our brains and so that it can carry the nutrients and proteins from our body to the brain. So, don't forget to drink enough water starting today!

8. No Exercise

Did you know that exercising not only improves your body but greatly helps in improving the functioning of your brain? So, how frequently do you exercise? You do not necessarily have to follow a rigorous routine or join a gym. It could be a swim in the pool from time to time or a jog in the morning. Exercising increases your heart rate, which then helps pump more oxygen to the brain. With the release of happy hormones known as endorphins, exercising also helps you remain younger. Not only that, but exercising is also known to produce and release other hormones that help the brain to grow and develop.

9. Overeating

Overeating is when you eat more than what your body needs. Eating too much is never a good idea as we all know the terrible consequences it brings about, such as an increase in weight, obesity, and cholesterol, among others. But among all this, did you know that overeating affects your brain too? It makes the arteries of your brains harder, leading to a decrease in mental power. Not only that, it creates an unhealthy cycle of overeating out of boredom, it also disrupts your sleeping habits, all of which cause stress and thus decrease your brain health more.

10. Working When Sick

Do not forget that your brain works the hardest, and so it is vital that you give it a rest. You can never get your brain back to its shape no matter how much you rest after you have overused it. Therefore, whenever you are sick, like having a headache or flu, or even when you are exhausted, do not push your brain to work. This will lead to a decrease in the effectiveness of the brain. If you have a habit of working like this, you are making your brain suffer severe and irreversible damage.

That brings us to the end of the ten habits that damage our brain. If you identified and related to one or more of these habits, then it is time that you remove them completely from your life so that you can preserve your most important body part - the brain, which also means protecting your whole body.

Chapter 3:

<u>10 Habits of Happy People</u>

Happy people live the most satisfying lives on the planet. They have come to understand the importance of not worrying because it will not make any differential change in their lives. If you cannot control the outcome of a process, why worry? If you can control and make a difference to the outcome of a situation, why worry? Worrying does not bring an ounce of success your way.

Here are 10 habits of happy people that could be you if you choose to adopt it:

1. <u>Happy People Count Their Blessings.</u>

Taking stock of your successes is an important part of appreciating yourself. You find comfort in knowing that despite all the hiccups you have found in your journey there remains an oasis of achievements in your desert.

Everyone needs to take stock of what is in his or her basket of blessings. It is a reminder of your resilience and persistence in the face of challenges. It is an indication of your ability and a minute representation of the progress you can make, given time.

Remind yourself of the taste of victory in your small achievements. It begins with understanding that you definitely cannot be able to win it all. There are grey and shadow areas that will not be within your reach.

2. Happy People Do Not Need the Validation of Others.

Happy people do not wait for the validation of other people. They are autonomous. Develop the habit of doing what is right regardless of your audience and you will have an authentic lifestyle. As such, your source of happiness will be independent of uncontrollable factors. Why should you tie your happiness to someone else capable of ruining your day in a snap? This is not to mean that you will not need other people. Humans are social beings and interdependent. Letting them strongly influence your lifestyle is the major problem. Be your own man.

3. They Are Bold.

Boldly and cautiously pursuing their ambitions is part of the ingredients that make up happy people. Knowing what you want is one thing and pursuing it is another. If music is your passion and it makes you happy, chase after it for it is therein that your happiness lies. Whatever it is (of course considering its legality) do not let it pass.

To be truly happy, do not live in the shadow of other happy people. Define your happiness and drink from your well. Timidity will make you bask under the shade of giants and create a sense of false security. One day the shade will be no more and leave you exposed to an unimaginable reality.

4. They are social people.

Being social is one common characteristic of happy people. Happiness makes them bubbly and alive. There is a common testament in almost all happy people – either happiness made them social or their social nature made them happy. Thanks to whichever of the two came earlier, they are happy people!

Like bad luck, happiness is contagious. Your social circle can infect you with happiness or even deny it to you. Being sociable does not mean to the extreme nature with all the hype that comes along.

It means being approachable to people. Some will positively add to your basket and others will offer positive criticism towards your cause. With such input, your happiness will have longevity.

5.   Believe in a greater cause.

Happy people understand that it is not always about them. There is a greater cause above their interests. They do not derive their happiness from the satisfaction of their needs and wants. Regardless of any deficiency in their lives, their flame of happiness is not easily put out.

Do you want to be happy? It is time to put self-interest aside and not tie your happiness to local anchors. An average person's happiness is mainly dependent on his well-being. Refusing to be average gives you leverage over those out to put off your happiness.

6.   Lead a purposeful life.

Are there happy people without purpose? Those we see happy maintain their status by having a powerful drive towards the same. A strong purpose will make you stay on happiness' lane. It is the habit of happy people to have a purpose. This is to enable them to stay on course.

Being happy is not a permanent state. It is easily reversible if caution is not taken. Purposefulness is part of the caution taken by happy people.

7. <u>Admit they are human.</u>

To err is human. Given this, happy people appreciate the erroneous nature of man and accept the things they cannot change, have the courage to change the things they can, and the wisdom to know the difference. A prayer commonly referred to as the serenity prayer.

Admitting being human is the first step towards being happy. You forgive yourself of your wrongs before seeking the forgiveness of another. This brings inner peace culminating in happiness.

8. <u>Know their strengths and weaknesses.</u>

Being aware of your strengths and weaknesses is one thing happy people have mastered. Through that, they know their limits; the time to push and time to take a break. This serves to help avoid unwarranted disappointments that come along with new challenges.

Nothing can put off the charisma of a prepared spirit. Happy people know their limitations well enough such that no ill-willed voice can whisper disappointments to them. They hold the power of self-awareness within their hearts making them live with contentment.

9. <u>Notice the contributions of those around them.</u>

No man is an island. The contributions of other people in our lives cannot be emphasized enough. We are because they are (for all the good reasons). At any one point in our lives, someone made us happy. The first step is noticing the roles played by those in our immediate environment.

The joy of being surrounded by people to hold our hands in life is engraved deeper in our hearts in times of need. It is time you stop looking far away and turn your eyes to see what is next to you.

10. <u>They are grateful and appreciative.</u>

"Thank you" is a word that does not depart from the lips of happy people. Their hearts are trained to focus on what is at their disposal instead of what they cannot reach. It is crystal that a bird in hand is worth two in the bush.

Happy people continue being happy despite deficiencies. Try being appreciative and see how happiness will tow along.

Adopt these 10 habits of happy people and depression will keep away from you. If you want to be happy, do what happy people do and you will see the difference.

Chapter 4:

8 Habits That Can Make You Happy

We're always striving for something, whether it's a promotion, a new truck, or anything else. This brings us to an assumption that "when this happens, You'll finally be happy."

While these important events ultimately make us happy, research suggests that this pleasure does not last. A Northwestern University study compared the happiness levels of ordinary people to those who had won the massive lottery in the previous years. It was found that the happiness scores of both groups were nearly equal.

The false belief that significant life events determine your happiness or sorrow is so widespread that psychologists have given it a name-"impact bias." The truth is that event-based happiness is transitory. Satisfaction is artificial; either create it or not. Long-term happiness is achieved through several habits. Happy people develop behaviors that keep them satisfied daily.

Here are eight habits that can make you happy.

1. Take Pride in Life's Little Pleasures.

We are prone to falling into routines by nature. This is, in some ways, a positive thing. It helps conserve brainpower while also providing comfort. However, it is possible to be so engrossed in your routine that you neglect to enjoy the little pleasures in life. Happy people understand the value of savoring the taste of their meal, revel in a great discussion they just had, or even simply stepping outside to take a big breath of fresh air.

2. Make Efforts To Be Happy.

Nobody, not even the most ecstatically happy people, wakes up every day feeling this way. They work harder than everyone else. They understand how easy it is to fall into a routine where you don't check your emotions or actively strive to be happy and optimistic. People who are happy continually assess their moods and make decisions with their happiness in mind.

3. Help other people.

Helping others not only makes them happy, but it also makes you happy. Helping others creates a surge of dopamine, oxytocin, and serotonin, all of which generate pleasant sensations. According to Harvard research, people who assist others are ten times more likely to be focused at work and 40% more likely to be promoted. According to the same study, individuals who constantly provide social support are the most likely to be happy during stressful situations. As long as you don't overcommit yourself, helping others will positively affect your mood.

4. Have Deep Conversations.

Happy people understand that happiness and substance go hand in hand. They avoid gossip, trivial conversation, and passing judgment on others. Instead, they emphasize meaningful interactions. You should interact with others on a deeper level because it makes you feel good, creates emotional connections, and, importantly, it's an intriguing way to learn.

5. Get Enough Sleep.

I've pounded this one too hard over the years, and I can't emphasize enough how important sleep is for enhancing your attitude, focus, and self-control. When you sleep, your brain recharges, removing harmful proteins that accumulate as byproducts of regular neuronal activity during the day. This guarantees that you awaken alert and focused. When you don't get enough quality sleep, your energy, attention, and memory all suffer. Even in the absence of a stressor, sleep loss elevates stress hormone levels. Sleep is vital to happy individuals because it makes them feel good, and they know how bad they feel when they don't get enough sleep.

6. Surround yourself with the right people

Happiness is contagious; it spreads through people. Surrounding yourself with happy people boosts your confidence, encourages your creativity, and is simply enjoyable.

Spending time with negative people has the opposite effect. They get others to join their self-pity party so that they may feel better about themselves. Consider this: if someone was smoking, would you sit there all afternoon inhaling the second-hand smoke? You'd step back, and you should do the same with negative people.

7. Always Stay Positive.

Everyone, even happy people, encounters difficulties daily. Instead of moaning about how things could or should have been, happy people think about what they are grateful for. Then they find the best approach to the situation, that is, dealing with it and moving on. Pessimism is a powerful source of sadness. Aside from the damaging effects on your mood, the problem with a pessimistic mindset is that it becomes a self-fulfilling prophecy. If you expect bad things, you are more likely to encounter horrific events. Gloomy thoughts are difficult to overcome unless you see how illogical they are. If you force yourself to look at the facts, you'll discover that things aren't nearly as awful as you think.

8. Maintain a Growth Mindset.

People's core attitudes can be classified into two types: fixed mindsets and growth mindsets. You believe you are who you are and cannot change if you have a fixed attitude. When you are challenged, this causes problems because anything that looks to be more than you can handle will make you feel despondent and overwhelmed. People with a growth mindset believe that with effort, they can progress. They are happy as a result of their improved ability to deal with adversity. They also outperform those with a fixed perspective because they welcome difficulties and see them as chances to learn something new.

Conclusion

It can be tough to maintain happiness, but investing your energy in good habits will pay off. Adopting even a couple of the habits on this list will have a significant impact on your mood.

Chapter 5:

6 Ways On How To Change Your Body Language To Attract Success

"If you want to find the truth, do not listen to the words coming to you. Rather see the body language of the speaker. It speaks the facts not audible." - Bhavesh Chhatbar.

Our body language is exceptionally essential as 60-90% of our communication with others is nonverbal. If properly used, it can be our key to more tremendous success. We focus more on our business plans, our marketing drives, and our spreadsheets rather than considering our facial expressions, posture, or what our physical gestures might be saying about us. Our mindset also plays a role in how our body language expresses itself. No matter how impressive our words maybe, if we are sending a negative signal with our body language, we would eventually lose the opportunities of gaining more success.

Here is a list to help you change your body language to attract more success.

1. The Power of Voice

Your personal voice has a huge impact and can literally make or break your success. It is one of the most direct routes to empower your communication. The pitch of your voice, its timbre, cadence, volume, and the speed with which you speak, are all influential factors that will ensure how convincing you are and how people will judge your character. Lowering your voice at the right moment or injecting some spontaneity into it when needed will enhance your credibility and lend you an air of intelligence. We must fill our voices with our range and depth if we want others and ourselves to take us seriously.

2. The Power of Listening

An excellent speaking skill represents only half of the leadership expression. The other half is mastering your art in listening. While a good listener is incredibly rare, it is essential to keep our ears open to any valuable information that is often silently transmitted. When we start listening attentively to others, we begin to notice what a person is saying and decode accurately what they don't say. You will also begin to realize what the other person is thinking or whether their attitude is positive or hostile towards you. With these particular observations, you will likely attune to another person and create the bond crucial to a successful working life.

3. The Necessity for Emotional Intelligence

The skill of acute listening develops our emotional intelligence, the intuition to ascertain the objective reality of the situation. When we lack emotional intelligence, we might misinterpret situations and fail to decipher what might be needed. Emotional intelligence deepens our empathy. It gives us the ability to be present and listen to someone when they need it the most. It is the single best predictor of performance in the workplace and can be the most vital driver of personal excellence and leadership. Our understanding of emotional intelligence will vastly improve our internal relations and can also deepen our sense of personal fulfillment and professional accomplishment.

4. The Power of Eye Contact

Making eye contact and holding it is seen as a sign of confidence, and the other person is felt valued. It increases your chance of being trustful and respected as they tend to listen to you more attentively and feel comfortable giving you their insights. You may be shy, an introvert, or might have heard that it's impolite to maintain eye contact with a superior. But in many parts of the world, business people expect you to maintain eye contact 50-60% of the time. Here's a simple tip: when you meet someone, look into their eyes long enough to notice their eye color.

5. Talk With Your Hands

There's a region in our brain called the Broca's area, which is essential and active during our speech production and when we wave our hands. Gestures are integrally linked to speech, so gesturing while talking can speed up your thinking. Using hand gestures while talking can improve verbal content as well as make your speechless hesitant. You will see that it will help you form clearer thoughts with more declarative language and speak in tighter sentences.

6. Strike A Power Pose

Research conducted at Harvard and Columbia Business Schools into the effects of body posture and confidence show that holding your body in expansive high-power poses (such as leaning back with hands behind the head or standing with legs and arms stretched wide open) for only as little as two minutes can stimulate high levels of testosterone (a hormone linked to power) and lower levels of cortisol (a stress hormone). You will look and feel more confident and inevitable, leading to an increased feeling of energy and a high tolerance for risk.

Conclusion

Most of our body language and movement are subconscious, so it can be challenging to retrain ourselves away from habits we have had for years. Still, we must try to master our body language, too, with the art of public speaking. Regular practice Is the key to success and the quickest route to attain confident body language as with any other skill. Practice them in your day-to-day life so that they may become deep-rooted. Be less compliant and step into an edgier, emboldened, and more genuine you.

Chapter 6:

5 Ways To Focus on Creating Positive Actions

Only a positive person can lead a healthy life. Imagine waking up every day feeling like you are ready to face the day's challenges and you are filled with hope about life. That is something an optimist doesn't have to imagine because they already feel it every day. Also, scientifically, it is proven that optimistic people have a lower chance of dying because of a stress-caused disease. Although positive thinking will not magically vanish all your problems, it will make them seem more manageable and somewhat not a big deal.

All you have to do is focus on the positive side of life. It is not necessarily true that people with a positive mindset always get disappointed. Positivity is like a breath of fresh air for us. Looking at the bright side of things has its advantages, and it has its very own benefits. So, positive energy is an essential factor to produce in oneself to make them more efficient in the ways of life. They tend to focus on all the good things and push aside all the wrong things, making them love everything they do.

1. Think Positively

Positive thinking is what leads to positive actions, actions that affect you and the people around you. When you think positively, your actions show how positive you are. You can create positive thinking by focusing on the good in life, even if it may feel tiny thing to feel happy about because when you once learn to be satisfied with minor things, you would think that you no longer feel the same amount of stress as before and now you would feel freer. This positive attitude will always find the good in everything, and life would seem much easier than before. You then become the person you once imagined yourself to be, just by thinking positively about it. So, make sure to process those positive thoughts thoroughly for better results or action.

2. Be Grateful

Being grateful for the things you have contributed a lot to your positive behavior. Gratitude has proven to reduce stress and improve self-esteem. Think of the things you are grateful for; for example, if someone gives you good advice, then be thankful to them, for if someone has helped you with something, then be grateful to them, by being grateful about minor things, you feel more optimistic about life, you feel that good things have always been coming to you. Studies show that making down a list of things you are grateful for during hard days helps you survive tough times. Also, be thankful to yourself for making achievements that you wanted. It makes you feel positive about yourself and makes your confidence boost through you. You have to make sure that you know what it is to be thankful for. Be grateful to someone for all the right reasons, and you will feel positive.

3. Laugh Through Situations

A person laughing always looks like a happy person. Studies have shown that laughter lowers stress, anxiety, and depression. Open yourself up to humor, permit yourself to laugh even if forced because even a forced laugh can improve your mood. Laughter lightens the mood and makes problems seem more manageable. Your laughter is contagious, and it may even enhance the perspective of the people around us. Smiling is free therapy. You have to pass an approving smile and make someone's day up.

4. Don't Blame Yourself For The Things You Can't Control

People with depression or anxiety are always their jailers; being harsh on themselves will only cause pain, negativity, and insecurity. So try to be soft with yourself, give yourself a positive talk regularly; it has proven to affect a person's actions. A positive word to yourself can influence your ability to regulate your feelings and thoughts. The positivity you carry in your brain is expressed through your actions, and who doesn't loves an optimistic person. Instead of blaming yourself, you can think differently, like "I will do better next time" or "I can fix this." Being optimistic about the complicated situation can lead your brain to find a solution to that problem.

5. Start Your Day with A dose of Positivity

When you wake up, it is good to do something positive in the morning, which mentally freshens you. You can start the day by reading a positive quote about life and understand the meaning of that quote, and you may feel an overwhelming feeling after letting the meaning set. Everybody loves a good song, so start by listening to a piece of music that gives you positive vibes, that gives you hope, and motivation for the day. You can also share your positivity by being nice to someone or doing something nice for someone; you will find that you feel thrilled and positive by making someone else happy.

Conclusion

Indeed, we can not just start thinking positively overnight, but we have to push ourselves more every time to improve. Surround yourself with brightness, good people, and a positive mindset—a good combination for a good life.

Chapter 7:

Five Habits That Make You Age Faster

We will all get old one day. A day is coming when we will not have the youthful energy we presently enjoy. Everyone desires that this day should never come or rather come very late in our lifetime. Nevertheless, it is an inevitable occurrence. We can only delay it.

Here are five habits that make you age faster:

1. Unforgiveness

Unforgiveness is like hiding fire expecting that no one will notice. Eventually, the smoke will give you away. It arises when one deeply wrongs us leaving a trail of hurt and agony that cannot easily be forgotten. The offended party will never forget what was committed against him/her. Anytime he/she sees the other person, the bad memory is re-kindled.

It is unhealthy to hold on to such bad memories. They cause mental and emotional trauma. They cause and affect your health. When your health is affected due to your unforgiveness, you bear full consequences and can only blame yourself. However subtle it may seem, unforgiveness is responsible for the fast aging of many people who harbor it.

The offender could probably have even forgotten about it and moved on with his/her life. The victim is the one who will be left bearing the brunt of the hurt. Stress will manifest on your face in the form of contortions making you appear aged than you are. Choose forgiveness always and you will lead a happier youthful life.

2.   Bitterness

Bitterness is an aftermath of unforgiveness. It is a very strong emotion that succeeds unforgiveness. Regardless that it springs forth from within, bitterness manifests on the face over time. The glory on the face of a joyous person is absent on that of a bitter person.

Ever asked yourself how people can judge someone's age bracket? The youthful glamour disappears on the face of a bitter person. Some elderly people appear very youthful. The reason is that they live a bitter-free life. Such a type of lifestyle guarantees youthfulness.

Strive to be youthful and live a fulfilling life by keeping bitterness at bay. Entertaining it will increase the rate at which you age and may succumb to old-age diseases while still at a very young age.

3.   Lack of Physical Exercise

Physical exercise is an important part of the human routine. It is not reserved for sports people only but everyone needs it to grow healthy. So important is exercise that it is incorporated in the education curriculum for students to observe.

Physical exercises help one become healthy and look youthful. It burns excess calories in our body and unblocks blood vessels thus increasing the efficiency of blood flow and body metabolism. Excess water, salts, and toxins are expelled from our bodies when we sweat after intense exercise.

The lack of physical exercise makes our bodies stiff and they become a fertile ground for lifestyle diseases like high blood pressure. Conversely, exercises improve our body shape and sizes by shedding extra weight. This healthy lifestyle brought by regular exercises will enable us to live a long healthy disease-free life.

4.   Poor Dieting

Dieting serves several purposes but the chief benefit of a proper dieting habit is that it gives the body important nutrients and shields it from excesses caused by human bias. Proper dieting will make you eat nutritive food that you may even not like. The benefits of nutritive meals outweigh your tastes and preferences.

Poor dieting is taking meals without considering their nutritive value or repetitively eating a meal because you love it. This habit makes you caution less with what you eat. You will ingest excess oily and fatty foods which will harm the healthy bacteria that live in your gut. It goes further to affect your heart health and immune response to diseases.

These factors directly affect the rate at which you age. Greasy foods will manifest in your skin and alter your appearance. It may also cause acne on your face. To reduce your aging rate, improve your dieting habit and supply the body with the right nutrients.

5.   Lack Of A Skincare Routine

As much as the skin is affected by the type of meals we take, a healthy skin care routine plays a major role in maintaining youthful skin. There are many celebrities globally who look younger than their age and this has a lot to do with their skincare routine.

It varies from one person to another but the fundamentals are constant - washing your face with plenty of clean water in the morning and evening. This is to remove dirt and dead cells from the skin. When one does not take care of his/her skin, aging creeps in. The face is the most visible part of the human body and it requires maximum care.

Failure to have an efficient skincare routine will entertain old age - the last item on our wish list.

Since we are now enlightened about habits that will make us age faster, the onus is on us to fight them and remain youthful.

Chapter 8:

4 Ways Geniuses Come Up with Great Ideas

Following are thumbnail descriptions of strategies common to the thinking styles of creative geniuses in science, art, and industry throughout history.

1. Geniuses Look at Problems in Many Different Ways

Genius often comes from finding a new perspective that no one else has taken. Leonardo da Vinci believed that to gain knowledge about the form of problems, you begin by learning how to restructure them in many different ways. He felt the first way he looked at a problem was too biased toward his usual way of seeing things. He would restructure his problem by looking at it from one perspective and move to another view and still another. With each move, his understanding would deepen, and he would begin to understand the essence of the problem. Einstein's theory of relativity is, in essence, a description of the interaction between different perspectives. Freud's analytical methods were designed to find details that did not fit with traditional perspectives to find a completely new point of view.

In order to creatively solve a problem, the thinker must abandon the initial approach that stems from past experience and re-conceptualize the problem. By not settling with one perspective, geniuses do not merely solve existing problems, like inventing an environmentally friendly fuel. They identify new ones. It does not take a genius to analyze dreams; it required Freud to ask in the first place what meaning dreams carry from our psyche.

2. Geniuses Make Their Thoughts Visible

The explosion of creativity in the Renaissance was intimately tied to the recording and conveying of a vast knowledge in a parallel language, a language of drawings, graphs, and diagrams — as, for instance, in the renowned diagrams of DaVinci and Galileo. Galileo revolutionized science by making his thought visible with charts, maps, and drawings, while his contemporaries used conventional mathematical and verbal approaches.

Once geniuses obtain a certain minimal verbal facility, they seem to develop a skill in visual and spatial abilities, which gives them the flexibility to display information in different ways. When Einstein had thought through a problem, he always found it necessary to formulate his subject in as many different ways as possible, including diagrammatically. He had a very visual mind. He thought in terms of visual and spatial forms rather than thinking along purely mathematical or verbal lines of reasoning. In fact, he believed that words and numbers, as they are written or spoken, did not play a significant role in his thinking process.

3. Geniuses Produce

A distinguishing characteristic of genius is immense productivity. Thomas Edison held 1,093 patents, still the record. He guaranteed productivity by giving himself and his assistants' idea quotas. His own personal quota was one minor invention every ten days and a major innovation every six months. Bach wrote a cantata every week, even when he was sick or exhausted. Mozart produced more than six hundred pieces of music. Einstein is best known for his paper on relativity, but he published 248 other papers. T. S. Elliot's numerous drafts of "The Waste Land" constitute a jumble of good and bad passages that eventually was turned into a masterpiece. In a study of 2,036 scientists throughout history, Dean Kean Simonton of the University of California, Davis found that the most respected produced great works and more "bad" ones. Out of their massive quantity of work came quality. Geniuses produce. Period.

4. Geniuses Make Novel Combinations

Dean Keith Simonton, in his 1989 book Scientific Genius suggests that geniuses are geniuses because they form more novel combinations than the merely talented. His theory has etymology behind it: cogito — "I think — originally connoted "shake together": intelligent the root of "intelligence" means to "select among." This is a clear early intuition about the utility of permitting ideas and thoughts to randomly combine with each other and the utility of selecting from the many the few to retain. Like the highly playful child with a pailful of Legos, a genius constantly combines and recombines ideas, images, and thoughts into different combinations in their conscious and subconscious minds. Consider Einstein's equation, $E=mc^2$. Einstein did not invent the concepts of energy, mass, or speed of light. Instead, by combining these concepts in a novel way, he could look at the same world as everyone else and see something different. The laws of heredity on which the modern science of genetics is based are the results of Gregor Mendel, who combined mathematics and biology to create new science.

Chapter 9:

Who Are You Working For?

Who you work for is up to you,

but ultimately every person has a choice in that decision.

Whether you are self-employed, self-made, or salaried,

You determine your own destiny.

As Earl Nightingale said, only the successful will admit it.

You might work for one company your whole life,

but ultimately you are still working for yourself and your family.

If you do not like the practices of your company,

you have the power to leave and make a change.

You must choose to serve who you believe to be worthy of your life.

High self-esteem stops successful people ever feeling subordinate to anyone.

Achieve your goals by envisioning yourself providing quality service in the companies

and places that will maximise your chances of success.

Always view yourself as equal to everybody.

All of us have unique talents and qualities within us.

Acknowledg that we can learn from anybody.

Nobody is above or below us.

You can build such qualities that are keys to success.

If one client is taking all your time, reassess his or her value.

If the contract is no longer rewarding, end it as soon as possible.

Doesn't matter if it is a business or personal relationship.

You must get clear on the fact that you are working for you.

You should consider no one your boss.

You should view whoever pays you as a client,

As such you should provide them the best service you can.

Always look to create more opportunity for your business.

Don't look for security - it doesn't exist.

Even if you find it for a time, I guarantee it will be boring at best.

Look for productivity and progression.

Change is definite. It is the only constant.

It will be up to you whether it is progression or regression.

Work with people who have similar goals and objectives.

You should always work with, never for.

Remember that you are always working for yourself.

If working with a company is not bringing you any closer to your goal,

End it now and find one that will.

You should never feel stuck in a job because leaving it is only a letter or phone call away.

You can replace that income in a million different ways.

If you don't like someone scheduling your week for you, start your own business.

If you don't know how, get the training.

Investing in your skills is an investment in your future.

Learning doesn't end with high school.

That was only the beginning – that was practice

Be a life-long learner.

Learn on the job.

Learn so you can achieve more.

Once you admit that you are working for you,
change your bosses title to 'client'.
Open your eyes to a world of other big and wonderful opportunities.

Realize that you are more valuable than you previously believed yourself to be.
Believe you will are incredibly valuable, and you deserve to be paid accordingly.

Whether you are a minimum wage worker or a company director,
you probably haven't even scratched the surface of your capabilities.

Every time someone places limits on what is possible, somebody proves them wrong.
You work for yourself, the possibilities are limitless.

Chapter 10:

Playing To Your Strengths

Have you ever asked yourself why you fail at everything you touch?

Why you seem to lack behind everyone you strive to beat?

Why you can't give up the things that are keeping you from achieving the goals you dream?

Has anyone told you the reason for all this?

You might wonder about it all your life and might never get to the right answer. Even though you stare at the answer every day in the mirror.

Yes! It's you! You are the reason for your failures.

You are the reason for everything bad going on in your life right now.

But you are also the master of your life, and you should start acting like one.

When the world brings you down, find another way to overcome the pressures.

Find another way to beat the odds.

Adverse situations only serve to challenge you.

Be mentally strong and bring the world to your own game.

Show the world what you are.

Show the world what you are capable of.

Don't let anyone dictate to you what you should do.

Rather shape your life to dictate the outcome with your efforts and skills.

You can't always be wrong.

Somewhere, and somehow, you will get the right answer.

That will be your moment to build what you lost.

That will be your moment to shut everyone else and rise high in the silence of your opponents.

If you don't get that chance, don't wait for it to come.

Keep going your way and keep doing the things you do best.

Paths will open to your efforts one day.

You can't be bad at everything you do.

You must be good at something.

Find out what works for you.

Find out what drives your spirit.

Find out what you can do naturally while being blind-folded with your hands tied behind your back.

There is something out there that is calling out to you.

Once you find it, be the best at it as you can.

It doesn't matter if you do not get to the top.

You don't anything to prove to anyone.

You only need one glimpse of positivity to show yourself that you have something worthwhile to live for.

Always challenge yourself.

If you did 5 hours of work today, do 7 tomorrow.

If you run 1 mile today, hit 3 by the end of the week.

You know exactly what you are capable of.

Play to your strengths.

Make it your motto to keep going every single day.

Make a decision.

Be decisive.

Stick with it.

Don't be afraid because there is nothing to fear.

The only thing to fear is the fear itself.

Tell your heart and your mind today, that you can't stop, and you won't stop.

Till the time you have the last breath in your lungs and the last beat in your heart, keep going.

You will need to put your heart out to every chance you can get to raise yourself from all this world and be invincible.

You have no other option but to keep going.

To keep trying until you have broken all the barriers to freedom.

You are unique and you know it.

You just need to have the guts to admit that you are special and live up to the person you were always meant to be.

Take stock of yourself today.

Where are you right now and where do you want to be?

The moment you realize your true goal, that is the moment you have unlocked your strengths.

Live your life on your terms.

Every dream that you dream is obtainable.

And the only way is to believe in yourself.

To believe that you are the only thing standing in the way of your past and your future.

Once you have started, tell yourself that there is no return.

Dictate your body to give up only when you have crossed the finish line.

Start acting on every whim that might get you to the ultimate fate.

These whims are your strength because you have them for a purpose.

Why walk when you can run?

Why run when you can fly?

Why listen when you can sing?

Why go out and dine when you can cook?

The biggest gift that you can give to yourself is the mental satisfaction that you provide yourself.

You are only limited to the extent you cage yourself.

The time you let go will be your salvation. But you have to let go!

CPSIA information can be obtained
at www.ICGtesting.com
Printed in the USA
LVHW050201130122
708310LV00019B/2361